Teaching the Church Today

By
Carl J. Pfeifer

TWENTY-THIRD PUBLICATIONS

POST OFFICE BOX 180   WEST MYSTIC, CONN. 06388

Library of Congress Catalog Card Number
78-51672
ISBN 0-89622-075-3

Cover by Dan Johnson
Joe Loverti
ART DIRECTION, INC.

Layout and design by Laurelyn Schmidt

Contents

DEDICATION

To my parents
who initiated me into the Church
and continue to show me
by their deep faith
and honest caring
what it means to be
a good Catholic,
a true Christian.

Editor's Preface

The Church? Who cares? We do! That is why we have put into a useful paperback, the excellent articles written for *Religion Teacher's Journal* by Carl J. Pfeifer.

This book has been designed and planned particularly for anyone who feels the need for immediate background reading before leading a group of people in an exploration, class, or discussion about the meaning of the Church. Here, you will find nine basic chapters which give historical and theological background on the Church using the basic "model" approach of Avery Dulles, S.J., plus the author's own "models."

As I edited this warm and intelligent book, I struggled with capitalization of the word "Church" when the reference obviously meant "people," no matter what the image or model under discussion. In doing this, I realized how very difficult it is to keep one clear image of the Church with a specific adjective. You will find the Church referred to as people, as "she" and as "it." If it were not for awkward construction, I would have preferred every reference to the Church to be "us"— first person, plural. As you become immersed in each chapter and its corresponding image of the Church, however, you will see how difficult it is to "pin down" one set of phrases. This difficulty confirms the truth that the mystery of the Church can only be approached through a wide multiplicity of models and images. Yet, all the while, there is the gnawing knowing that not even a collection of images or models can sufficiently reflect the total mystery of the Church.

Because so many are called upon these days to relate to people of all ages and levels of understanding, the author has added a variety of teaching and learning activity suggestions at the end of each chapter which can be used or adapted for little children, intermediates, teens, and adults. In fact, where intergenerational programs are in progress, the various groups can be encouraged to participate in learning about the same theme.

Carl Pfeifer's love for the Church and his disciplined integration of biblical, historical, theological, cultural and psychological information about the Church comes through in a very easy-to-read-and-understand style. Besides his own insights as the result of years of study, teaching, and writing, he has added a list of suggestions at the end of each chapter for further reading from other sources as well as resource materials available for classroom and other learning settings.

What this book accomplishes, it seems to me, is the comforting of people who read it, for each will identify with one or more of the images or models of the Church and discover richer reasons for gratitude for being called to be the Church. And, although we edited this book with the presumption in mind that you would be using it as background reading and study for your own class or discussion presentation on the Church, I know that personally, I plan to send copies to many people whom, I know, will appreciate the answers provided here to many of their unarticulated but very real questions.

—Marie McIntyre

Introduction

I grew up in St. Louis during the 30's and 40's. Everyone I knew was Catholic, and except for my parents, the German cook at the convent, and the Italian cop on our beat, all the Catholics I knew were Irish. Our neighborhood surrounded Blessed Sacrament Church and school. Everyone I knew belonged to Blessed Sacrament parish.

Our German bakery was just across Kingshighway Boulevard from the Church. Irish bread was one of our best selling items. Sunday morning was just about our busiest time of the week. People from the neighborhood dropping in for bakery goods after Mass was a delightful part of the Sunday ritual.

Those were peaceful, happy times, as I remember them. Louis Bruzatti, our police patrolman, spent many a quiet Sunday afternoon cooking spaghetti for us— leaving from time to time to call into the police station to assure them that all was well in the neighborhood. Few people ever moved in or out of the neighborhood. Life was stable, predictable. Nothing that happened was ever far from the Church, as a physical building dominating our neighborhood, as an institution to which we all belonged.

None of us had any question about what a Catholic was. We knew some were better Catholics than others. Dozens dropped into our bakery every morning for breakfast rolls after attending daily Mass. Others dropped in accidentally, unable to stagger straight home from the Corkscrew, the neighborhood tavern next door. We all knew that good Catholics went to Mass on Sunday, confession at least once a year, ate fish on Friday, did not date Protestants, supported the Church financially and obeyed its laws.

We obeyed the Pope in everything involving faith and morals. What the Pope had to say, we learned mostly from Msgr. Marron, who was pastor as long as I could remember. His word was law. No one doubted that if Monsignor said it, the Church taught it. And from time to time Archbishop Glennon sent a letter to be read at Sunday Mass. He made it clear what the Church taught on particularly difficult issues.

If someone had asked us what was the Church, we might not have remembered exactly the words of the Baltimore Catechism, but our answer would have been close to the mark.

Q. *What is the Church?*

A. *The Church is the congregation of all those who profess the faith of Christ, partake of the same sacraments, and are governed by their lawful pastors under one visible head.*

The "faith of Christ" was what we learned from the Baltimore Catechism. The "sacraments" were the well-known seven. Msgr. Marron was our lawful pastor and Pope Pius XI was the "one visible head." The "congregation of all" comprised a clearly defined "perfect society" which contained all the means necessary for salvation. It was all quite clear. It was relatively simple. And our experience matched the definition.

In fact, centuries of experience meshed easily with that definition. It was written 400 years earlier by Cardinal Robert Bellarmine in only slightly differing words: "The one and true Church is the community of men brought together by the profession of the same Christian faith and conjoined in the communion of the same sacraments, under the government of the legitimate pastors and especially the one vicar on earth, the Roman Pontiff." His definition lasted so long because it fit what people, like us in Blessed Sacrament Parish in St. Louis 30 years ago, knew the Church to be from our own experience.

The definition was neat and clear. It described observable, external traits. With it, you could distinguish Catholics from all other believers. From it, you gathered what you had to do to be a Catholic. The Baltimore Catechism simply filled out the details implied in the definition. From it we knew what Catholics were to believe, how they were to worship and live.

Big Change

Since those peaceful days the world and the Church have suffered a series of shocks. The old neighborhood is no more the same than is Blessed Sacrament parish. The cultural and ecclesial upheavals of the sixties have shattered our clear, precise definitions by fracturing the stable, uniform experience of society and church which gave apparent validity to the definitions.

There is no need to catalogue the dramatic changes in the Catholic Church since Vatican Council II. We have lived through them. There is no space here to list the legitimate differences, the honest pluralism, among Catholics that replace the equally honest uniformity of our earlier experience. The Church I knew in St. Louis in the 40's was strikingly—and for the most of us in one way or another, painfully—different from the Church I know today.

Just as different is our understanding of the Church. Relatively few would be completely comfortable with the definition of Bellarmine and Baltimore. Whereas it was once helpful, and true to our experience, today it is sadly inadequate. Already before Vatican II, Pope Pius XII had shifted focus from "perfect society" to "mystical body." He pointed to the inner spiritual reality of the institution. But the shape of the institution tended to remain the same. Today, however, a monolithic Church, with all authority and teaching descending from one Supreme Pontiff, with all the faithful thinking, speaking and acting uniformly in matters of faith and morals, no longer exists. Some bemoan its demise, while others dance on its grave.

The transition has been painful for almost everyone. Confusion, polarization, anger, frustration and apathy characterize our changed, still changing, and pluralistic church. But the pain has not been without profound benefits. One of these must surely be the recognition that the Church is tremendously more mysterious, interesting, challenging, demanding, frustrating, fulfilling, exciting and spiritual than the pre-Vatican II clear, precise, legalistic definition of Church suggests. The Church eludes the grasp of our cataloguing, defining efforts. It is much richer than the "perfect society" image of Bellarmine and subsequent theology and catechesis. It is alive, vibrant, growing—not just with human life—but with the creative vitality of Christ's life-enhancing Spirit.

The Bishops at the Second Vatican Council came to sense this. Rejecting an overly organizational definition of the Church, they focused on the Church as "mystery." They searched back centuries beyond Baltimore and Bellarmine to the Scriptures and the early Fathers of the Church. They recovered the long lost—but curiously contemporary—awareness of the *mystery* of Church. Mystery suggests the always unnameable, untameable presence of the divine. Mystery consistently eludes categorization. Mystery forever belies clear, precise definition. It breaks the boundaries of human logic, and stretches human language to its limits—ultimately to awesome silence before the divine. Mystery is the realm more of poetry than of philosophy; it is the domain of the childlike.

Description
Not Definition

As a result of the emphasis on mystery, the Council chose to follow the lead of the Scriptures. Recognizing the mysterious reality of the Church, the Council proceeds not so much to clearly define it as did Bellarmine and the Council of Trent, but rather to describe it in a variety of images. Jesus similarly spoke in poetic imagery of the kingdom of God, as the prophets before Him spoke symbolically about God's people. In its Constitution on the Church, the Council, echoing the Bible, speaks of the Church as a sheepfold, a flock, the field of the Lord, a vineyard, the edifice of God, the temple, the New Jerusalem, a mother, a bride, the mystical body of Christ, a society, a people, a pilgrim, an exile.

The almost embarrassing number of images suggests something of the always ungraspable reality they attempt to describe. Bellarmine's clear, precise definition tended to close off further probing of the mystery of the Church. As symbolic expression, the biblical and conciliar images do just the opposite. They provide insight while evoking further contemplation. Each is limited, needing others to balance it. They are not logically cohesive. How can a bride be a vineyard, a city, a pilgrim, a temple, a mother? In the logically abstract language of symbol and poetry, they are mutually enriching.

For some years theologians, like Avery Dulles, have refined the abundant imagery of Bible and Council. They speak not so much of a clear-cut, measurable definition of the Church, as they do of "models" of the Church. Models provide insight into reality, but suggest new dimensions still to be explored. The terminology is related to the modern scientific use of models to explain existing data and to open up more fruitful lines of future experimentation. In a sense, the theologians' "models" are simply more refined versions of the biblical "images." They interpret the data of "Church" and point out further avenues of probing its mysterious reality.

Many Models

The present book attempts to share with catechists, parents and others, the approach to understanding the Church by means of theological models. To those more comfortable with philosophic definition, like that of the Baltimore Catechism, the present symbolic descriptions may at first be disappointing, appearing vague, inconclusive. Undoubtedly much more work needs to be done in reflecting on and refining the models used to explore the mystery of the Church while considerably more philosophical reflection is needed as well. But the existing philosophic definition with which most of us at one time were comfortable is simply inadequate. It no longer expresses either the Church's understanding of itself as reflected in Vatican Council II, or reflects the reality of the contemporary Church as we experience it.

Avery Dulles lists and explores five "models," namely, *Institution, Mystical Communion, Sacrament, Herald,* and *Servant.* He admits that many other models are possible. We will explore his and several more. As Avery Dulles observes, not every model is of equal value or importance. But, if valid at all, each of the models of the Church will provide rich insight into the reality of the Church as it is and ought to be as well as open up fruitful leads to further discoveries about the Church.

Msgr. Marron is long dead, as is Cardinal Glennon and Pope Pius XI and Pius XII. The Church we experienced with them no longer exists with its secure stability and uniformity. Bellarmine's definition of Church served that experience of the Church well for some centuries. Without ingratitude to any of them, we need to attempt to understand a Church much more elusive, more pluralistic, more voluntary, more democratic; in a word, more obviously mysterious.

"You are the body of Christ and individually members of it. So, if you are the body of Christ and the members thereof, then it is your own mystery which lies on the altar of the Lord; it is the mystery of yourselves which you receive. You reply 'Amen' to what you are; by that reply you confirm this fact. For when on receiving the body you hear 'The body of Christ,' you answer 'Amen.' Therefore, you must really be a member of the body of Christ so that your Amen may be true."

—*St. Augustine (PL38, 1246-8)*

Jeff Brass

1

The Church as the Context of our Faith

"I've had it with the Church, but I still believe in God. And, curiously, I want my kids to grow up Catholic."

My friend's words have given me pause for much thought. They echo similar feelings of parents I've met at religious education meetings around the country.

"I grew up knowing exactly what a Catholic was supposed to believe and do," said another parent friend. *"Today, I'm so confused. I don't even know what to tell my own children. I sometimes wonder that I still believe in God!"*

For thousands of parents and catechists—and priests and religious—the Church has become a source of questioning, doubt, even disbelief. Many Catholics experience a frightening gap between what they thought to be their unshakable faith in God and their very shaken belief in the Church. Claiming to be a living sign of faith in God, the Church appears to some to be a countersign.

Whatever one believes to be the cause of the crisis, the crisis in the Church is real and is closely related to people's faith. In fact, a "faith crisis" is often more truly a "Church crisis."

Painful as it is, the present unsettled situation appears to me to be basically healthy. Questioning and dissatisfaction challenge us to rethink the relationship between our faith in God and our belief in the Roman Catholic Church.

The present situation is not unlike the crisis the Hebrews faced when they found themselves in captivity in Babylon. The exile in Babylon was a time of radical faith crisis, closely tied with a crisis of religious institutions. Every traditional sign or symbol of God's promise and presence had been laid open to question. God had promised to be with the Hebrews in their own land; but that land was occupied by idolators, while they sat weeping in exile. God had promised to be with them in the Temple at Jerusalem but the Temple had been burned to the ground. God had said He would be with them in their king, a successor of King David, but their king had been deposed and deformed. It seemed to them that their covenant with God had been broken. They who had prided themselves on being God's people were no longer a "people," but a disillusioned band of exiles.

Yet, surprisingly, it was in that time of crisis that the great prophets of Israel—Isaiah, Jeremiah, Ezekiel—sparked a profound spiritual and institutional renewal. They assured the people that God was still reliable. His promises could be trusted. His presence embraced them even in exile. The prophets proclaimed there would be a new land, a new king, a new temple, a new covenant, a new people. The God of Abraham, Moses and David remained their God.

The great prophets of Israel jarred the dispirited people into realizing that their faith must be in God who is greater than any sign or symbol of God, no matter how sacred or traditional it might be. Faith in the one, true God might well find nourishment in sacred signs, but the signs must never be equated with God. Nothing but the living God was to be the object of people's total trust or faith. They were called to place their lives in the hands of God, not of the organized religious institution.

Faith in God Alone

The present crisis in the Church appears quite similar to that of the Jews in exile. Many of the traditional signs of God's promises and presence have changed or all but disappeared. The uniformity of doctrinal expression, moral judgment and liturgical worship has given way to a rich pluralism. Many of us grew up seeing worldwide uniformity as a sign of God's presence with us, the one, true Church. We knew the Church was "one" because everywhere we went we experienced the same ritual, language, and lifestyle. Stability was another sign for us of God's unchanging presence. But the stability has given way to change and development, even to some insecurity.

The ecclesial signs of unity, stability and security are no longer so clear or convincing. Like the exiled Israelites, we are thrown back on the heart of the prophetic message, which is also that of Jesus. God and God alone is the object of faith. Nothing, not even the Church, can be believed in as if it were God. As St. Thomas Aquinas taught some 800 years ago, our faith rests in God—not in doctrinal teachings, Church structures, or liturgical rituals.

We place our total trust in God alone, mysteriously mighty, tenderly gracious, ultimately eluding all that can be said about Him, embracing us in our innermost depths. *Faith, for faithful Jew and Christian, is first and foremost an experienced trust in and commitment to a God who is as gracious as He is great.*

In that sense, we cannot believe in the Church, the Pope, Catholic doctrine or the Bible. They are essential but inadequate means of expressing our faith, preserving it, trying to make sense out of it, and celebrating it. In fact, the very shattering of our previous securities in the Church and its teachings can be a healthy catalyst of a deeper faith in God. Like the exiled Jews, many modern Catholics are finding new faith in God and His Son, Jesus, as the religious signs of that faith seem to be crumbling. It is not surprising that the present institutional crisis within the Church is marked by a significant revival of prayer and spirituality.

Yet there is a real sense in which true faith in God is intimately linked with belief in and attachment to a community of believers or a Church. Like the Jews in exile, we believe not in an aloof, disinterested Power, but in a mighty God whose love for us envelops our life and world. Rooted in such a belief, the great prophets of Israel urged the people to renew their traditional symbols and institutions. Isaiah and Jeremiah did not urge the people to forget or reject their religious traditions, but to return to them as a source and expression of their faith in the one God of their ancestors. The prophets proclaimed a new people, ruled by a new king, bound to a new covenant, living in a new land, with a new Temple at its center.

So also today, the crisis of belief in the Church can lead not only to a deeper faith in God as the sole source of security and salvation, but to a renewed understanding of and commitment to the Church. From the days of Peter and Paul, those who placed their lives in the hands of God, the Father of Jesus Christ, united together in fellowship. Local groups of believers who called God, "our Father," met regularly in one another's homes as brothers and sisters to renew and celebrate their faith. These local communities or Churches linked themselves with other Churches. Gradually, a world-wide network of Churches arose, "catholic" in that it was open to the whole world.

Church as the Context of Our Faith

The Church was the normal context in which people deepened their faith in God, their Father, and in Jesus, His Son. The Church remains today the natural soil in which people's faith in God and Jesus is meant to sink its roots and draw nourishment. Solitary faith is abnormal. Even the ancient hermits in the desert preserved ties with the nearby Christian communities. Faith seeks community. Believers need fellow believers. The Church is the natural context of faith.

The normal growth of Christian faith in Jesus and His

Father is toward involvement in the Christian community of those who share that same faith. When the two despondent disciples recognized the Risen Lord in the "breaking of the bread" at Emmaus, they rejoined the community of disciples in Jerusalem (Luke 24:33). When Philip led the puzzled Ethiopian to faith in Jesus, he immediately baptised him into the community of believers (Acts 8:26-38). From the earliest days of the Church, faith was sealed by Baptism, confirmed, and then celebrated in the Eucharist. These community rituals became known as "sacraments of initiation" into the Church and "signs of faith."

The Second Vatican Council has drawn attention to the vital bond between faith in Jesus and involvement in the Church as the normal context for growth in faith. In its wake, the recent *Revised Rite of Christian Initiation for Adults* sets out challenging guidelines for restoring the catechumenate—a lengthy process of initiation into the ideals and lifestyle of the local community of believers. The assumption underlying this process is that the local Church is the normal place for faith in God and Jesus to develop. It is meant to be a particularly graced environment for faith growth.

As such, the Church is also, in a limited sense, something to believe in. Not in the sense that the Church or anyone or anything in it is to be trusted as one trusts only God, but in the sense that the mysterious God mysteriously unites Himself with the Church. St. Paul goes so far as to call the Church the "body of Christ" and the "temple of the Holy Spirit." St. John has Jesus promise that the Father and He will abide with His friends. He is the vine of which they are branches.

The Church can never take the place of God in our lives. He alone can be the ultimate source of meaning and life. But God, who became flesh for us, remains incarnate in the Church. Faith in the God of Jesus is traditionally linked with belief in the Church, whose members become one body, the Body of Christ. In that sense, we can pray in the Apostles' Creed that we "believe in the holy, Catholic Church."

Such is the ideal. For many today, however, what should be the normal relation of faith and Church appears the abnormal exception. The Catholic who struggles to trust God more and more in daily life should normally expect to experience a parallel growth in belief in the Church. But as my friends, quoted earlier, indicate, that is not always the case. Problems with the Church seem too often to stifle or strangle faith in God, or stimulate faith in God while leading to apathy with or resentment of the Church. In any event, today's crisis of faith and crisis with the Church are closely related.

A Challenge to Catechists

The very real tension between faith in God and belief in the Church as widely experienced today creates a serious challenge to the pastoral mission of the Church as well as to individual faith. In reflecting on our experience of God and our experience of the Church, we need to explore seriously our understanding of the Church. How we understand the Church affects not only our personal lives, but also the structure and priorities of our parishes and the approaches we adopt in our work as catechists—at home as parents, in the pulpit as priests, or in the classroom as religious educators.

As Catholics who place our faith in an incarnate God Who draws people together with Him and with one another, no honest coming to grips with our faith in God or our catechetical ministry can avoid a hard look at what we think of the Church. Whether we experience the Church today as a marvellous sign of faith or as a distressing sign of contradiction to a living faith, we avoid dealing with the Church only at the risk of diluting our faith in the God of Jesus Christ, our Father and His.

SUGGESTED ACTIVITIES

Primary Level

1. *Tour Church:* Take the children on a tour of their parish church. Help them notice everything in the church that is meant to help the people grow in their faith, for example, space to gather as a community, the altar, tabernacle, crucifix, statues, stations, paintings, stained glass windows, candles, etc. Help them sense that the church is a place for people to celebrate and deepen their knowledge and love of God. Let the children look at and touch and question whatever interests them. Lead them in periodic brief moments of prayer as you go around the church building.

2. *Participate in a Baptism:* Invite the children to participate in an actual Baptism in their parish. Prepare them beforehand. Then let them share in the baptismal celebration. Immediately afterwards, encourage them to ask questions about anything about which they are curious. If participation in an actual Baptism is not possible, then take them to the baptismal font in their parish church and show them the font, the water, ritual and bible, candle, white robe, etc. Explain each object briefly and simply, in relation to the sacrament as an initiation into the church community. Sing a simple song together and pray briefly.

3. *Creative drawing:* Provide the children with drawing or painting materials. Ask them to draw themselves in the center of the paper. Have them then draw all around them people who make up the church for them: parents, friends, neighbors, relatives, parish priest, perhaps even the local bishop and the pope. When they finish, have them display and talk about their creative work. Help them appreciate—and perhaps pray for—the Church in which they are growing up.

Intermediate Level

1. *Explore Baptismal Rite:* Guide the youngsters in exploring the rite of Baptism. Center their attention on the symbolic actions and on the more important prayers. Creative projects might be designed to help them explore the symbolism of water (symbol of life and of death as well as of cleansing), of light, and of new white garments. One or more of the biblical readings from the ritual could be read, discussed, and related to their creative exploration of the ritual symbols.

2. *Interview Adults:* Suggest that the youngsters develop several questions for interviewing their parents or other adult relatives and friends. The questions should focus on what being a Catholic means to them, why they are members of the Church, what difference being in the Church makes on their faith. After taking the interviews, the students should share the results with one another. Guide them in discussing their findings and their reactions to what they have discovered.

3. *Study Saints:* Have the youngsters study the lives of more relevant and appealing saints—or great non-canonized Christians like Tom Dooley, Dorothy Day, Cesar Chavez, Mother Teresa, or exemplary Catholics in their own community. Help them grow in a sense of pride in being related in the Church to such great Christians. Guide them in recognizing how these men and women grew up within the Church community and in turn helped the Church grow in faith and love.

Secondary Level

1. *Select photos:* Divide the group into teams of four to six. Allow at least 30 minutes. Each individual selects from a supply of photos—any subject matter—one that best conveys what he or she thinks and feels about the Church. Share photos, ideas and feelings in teams.

Teams then each select the one photo they feel is most representative. Teams now share with whole group. Help the group to agree on the one most representative photo.

2. *Write opinions:* Read the quotations which begin this chapter and ask the students to write their own ideas and feelings about their faith and their Church. Volunteers may share what they wrote and discussion can follow.

3. *React to Media:* Select a stimulating media presentation such as *Will the Real Church Please Stand Up?*, or *Windows* (See the RESOURCES list). Share it with the group. Give time afterwards for individual and/or small group discussion. Then guide the whole group in reacting to the media presentation in the light of their own experiences, ideas and feelings about the Church and faith. If time and interest permit, challenge them to create their own media presentation on the Church as the context of their faith.

Adult Level

1. *Work in groups:* Guide the group in a creative exploration of what "Church" means to them. Allow an hour or hour and a half. Begin with a few moments of quiet time, during which each person reflects on his or her own experience. They then write in their own words what they mean by "Church."

Then form working teams of 4 to 6 persons each. Give each team a large sheet of newsprint or an overhead transparency (and appropriate writing materials). Give them a threefold task:

  a. *Share:* Talk together about what "Church" means to you.
  b. *Create a symbol:* As they share, they are to work toward a consensus as to a symbol or

picture they feel best expresses what they mean by "Church." They draw the symbol or picture on the paper or transparency.

c. *Define:* Then they are to agree on a verbal definition of "Church" as they understand it. The brief definition is then written on the same paper or transparency as their symbol.

When the teams are ready, they share with the entire group what they have created. A spokesperson from each team explains and answers questions. Challenge them to find biblical, liturgical or doctrinal parallels to their own symbols and definitions.

End with a prayer experience flowing out of their creative work.

2. *Discuss:* Provide the group with such questions as: *What are my honest feelings about the Church? What does my experience of the Church have to do with my faith in God, in Jesus? Why? What do I feel would make my parish Church a more vital influence on my faith in God? What can I do to share my faith with others so as to improve the quality of parish community life?* Have them form teams of 4 to 6 persons. Ask them to discuss one or more of the questions in terms of their own experiences, feelings and ideas. Someone in each group should take notes and be prepared to present the team's ideas and feelings to the whole group.

Teams then report their responses to the questions to the entire group. Guide the group in further discussion, helping them note any similarities or differences between the teams' reactions.

Afterwards, have them compare results of the discussions with their own earlier reactions.

3. *Write Creeds:* Ask individuals to take time to think of what they as Catholic Christians really believe.

Have them write their own personal creed, beginning "I believe. . . ."

Encourage them to share their creeds, reading and explaining them to the whole group.

Afterwards as a meditation play Joe Wise's, "Creed," on his record, *A New Day* or "I Believe in You" on his record, *Close Your Eyes . . . I Got a Surprise.* (North American Liturgy Resources, 2110 W. Peoria Ave., Phoenix, Az. 85029).

4. *Pray Apostles' Creed:* Give out copies of the Apostles' Creed. Pray it aloud together. Encourage those who do not know it to learn it by heart.

RESOURCES

Will the Real Church Please Stand Up?. 7½ min. 33 ⅓ record with guide. (TeleKETICS, 1229 South Santee Street, Los Angeles, Ca. 90015). A sound collage of people's voices expressing their impressions of "Church."

Windows. 7½ min. color filmstrip (TeleKETICS, 1229 South Santee Street, Los Angeles, Ca. 90015). Sound and photo guide as explanation of the paradoxes of tradition/change, institution/individual, and divine/human.

Photomeditations, by Carl J. Pfeifer. 20 color slides (Mark IV Presentations, La Salette, Attleboro Ma. 02703). Printed meditations and discussion guide accompany slides to explore moments of life in the light of faith.

Photomeditations, by Carl J. Pfeifer. Photos and words explore life's mystery in the light of Christian faith and tradition. (Thomas More Assn. 180 N. Wabash Ave., Chicago, Ill. 60601)

Wonder. Faith. Present Moment. Prayer. Very short (about 2 minutes each) films for reflection on God's involvement in life. (Ikonographics, Inc., P.O. Box 4454, Louisville, Ky. 40204).

They Shall See. A 5-minute film meditation probing the mystery of life through the eyes of faith. (TeleKET-ICS, 1229 South Santee Street, Los Angeles, Ca. 90015).

READINGS

Avery Dulles, S.J., *Models of the Church* (New York: Doubleday, 1974). A basic book for exploring various models of understanding the Church.

Avery Dulles, S.J., *The Resilient Church* (New York: Doubleday, 1977). Explores the limits and necessity of adaptation in the Church.

Richard McBrien, *The Remaking of the Church* (New York: Harper & Row, 1973). The first half of the book presents a helpful diagnosis of reasons for present crises in the Church.

Andrew Greeley, *The New Agenda* (New York: Doubleday, 1973). Helpful for discerning reasons for different approaches to Church's beliefs and practices.

William Rademacher, *Answers for Parish Councils* (West Mystic, Ct: Twenty-Third Publications, 1974). See final chapter on theology of Church for capsule explanation of Vatican II's Document on the Church.

James Anderson, *To Come Alive! A New Proposal for Revitalizing the Local Church* (New York: Seabury Press, 1973). A practical, positive approach to parish life.

Monika Helwig, *The Christian Creeds* (8121 Hamilton Ave., Dayton, Ohio: Pflaum, 1973). A helpful analysis of the Church's basic creeds. Also related is her book, *Tradition—The Catholic Story* (Dayton, Ohio: Pflaum, 1974).

Janaan Manternach and Carl J. Pfeifer, *A Case for Faith* (Morristown, N.J.: Silver Burdett, 1978). Explores reasons for faith through significant human experiences and world religions. *A Case for Christianity* (Silver Burdett, 1978) traces the major traditions of Christianity.

Gregory Baum, *Journeys* (Ramsey, N.J., Paulist Press, 1976). Autobiographical statements of leading theologians on how experience shapes their understanding of their faith.

Carl J. Pfeifer and Janaan Manternach, *Living Water—Prayers of Our Heritage* (New York: Paulist Press, 1978). A beautifully illustrated collection of traditional prayers, with simple explanations of their meaning and place in the prayer life of the Church.

Carl Pfeifer

2

The Church as a Pilgrim People

They came that evening, about 25 parents and catechists, to hear me lecture on religious education. They thought I could tell them how to teach their children religion. They sat in orderly rows facing the speaker's podium, behind which I stood. A blackboard was on my left. The pastor sat to my right.

As I nervously shuffled my notes, they gazed expectantly at me. I looked at them. I glanced around the room. I acted uncomfortable. "I'm not sure how you feel," I began, "but I'm a bit uncomfortable about the way this room is set up. I wonder what it suggests about what you might be expecting here this evening."

Embarrassed silence. Then a man anxiously said he and his wife wanted me, an expert, to tell them how they could do a better job to rear their children as Catholics.

I returned again to the room arrangement. "Let's look more closely at this room. What does the way it is arranged suggest about the Church?" They were beginning to become uncomfortable. Several were obviously angry. Testily, a gentleman said it looked like the Church he always knew, organized to allow a priest or some other expert to tell lay people what is right or wrong. Others chimed in. "The Church is a perfect society with the hierarchy at the top—that's what I learned in college." "We want to know what the Church teaches. That's why we came here tonight!"

The climate was heating up. Vehement disagreements surfaced. "We're the Church, not just the clergy." "I think we also have something to say. Priests might listen sometimes." As the discussion got more intense, I interjected: "Let's stop for a moment. Why don't we get rid of this podium and blackboard. We might move our chairs into a circle." They reluctantly picked up the chairs, formed a circle and sat down. I joined them as part of the circle. So did the pastor. Some were obviously delighted. Others painfully frustrated. A few were furious.

"How do you like this new arrangement?" I asked. "What does it suggest about the Church?"

An hour-long, intense discussion followed. Opinions were strong, impressions mixed, feelings deep. Two models of the Church clearly emerged: one, a triangle or pyramid—like the original room arrangement; the other, a circle—like the second arrangement. The first focused on clergy, (and the clergy's guest expert) the second on people, everyone.

Church as People

It was a difficult but rewarding evening. We experienced in miniature what the Church as a whole has been living through since the Second Vatican Council. Having grown up with an impression of the Church as a "perfect society," an institution possessing all the necessary truths and means of salvation—which we received from the clergy—we were less than comfortable with a view of the Church as people searching together for ever greater insights into life's mysteries. After all, a pyramid is more stable than a circle. *A circle can roll.*

Vatican Council II took a predominantly circular view of the Church. Without in any way denying the institutional nature of the Church and the vital role of the hierarchy, the Council spoke primarily of the Church as God's "People." The focus in such an image or model of the Church is on community more than institution, on spirituality more than structure. Wisdom, insight, truth, healing, spiritual experience and counsel may be expected from anyone, no matter what his or her position in the Church. All have unique gifts from the Holy Spirit. All therefore deserve respect and a sensitive hearing. All have responsibilities for the whole Church.

The Council's emphasis on the Church as "God's People," is evidently influenced by the worldwide democratic trends of our time, with their emphasis on human rights and dignity. But it is also rooted in the soundest traditions of Judaeo-Christian experience.

Church in the New Testament

The New Testament built upon, developed and transposed the dominant concept of the "People of God" in the Hebrew Scriptures. Moses' words at Sinai (Ex 19:6) are recalled as the First Letter of Peter describes the early Christian communities as "a chosen race, a royal priesthood, a holy nation, a people He (God) claims for His own . . . Once you were no people, but now you are God's people" (1 Pt 2:9-10). Jeremiah prophesied a new people with a new covenant (Jer 31:31-34). His words are picked up to describe the Church in the Letter to the Hebrews, whose author has God say: "I will be their God and they shall be my people" (Heb 8:10).

St. Paul also speaks of the Church as God's new people, but he seems to favor the image or model of the "body of Christ." Paul stresses that all are members of the same body, each with unique gifts (Rom 12:3-8). Each person's giftedness is given to help the whole body, in which every member is important and deserving of respect (1 Cor 12:1-31). The only "head" is Jesus Christ, to whom all owe obedience and love. Other authorities are primarily gifted to serve the whole community which is to grow through mutual support and love (Eph 4:1-16).

Both biblical models—People of God, and Body of Christ—highlight two characteristics of the Church: fellowship or community, and spirituality. The New Testament descriptions of the early Church show a strong sense of fellowship or community, *koinonia.* At first, at least in Jerusalem, the intense community sense embraced even mutual financial support (Acts 3:42-47; 4:32-37; 5:12-16). The local churches were in fact communities of those who believed in Jesus Christ as Lord and Savior. But the fellowship of believers, no matter how deep and all-embracing, was very human and pluralistic. There were differences, culturally and theologically. There were even divisions at times and disputes. There was a richness of diversified gifts and graces. The unity was not one of uniformity, but of rich—and often painful—sharing of individual resources and convictions.

Something of this sense of deep fellowship abounding in individual differences of talent and grace is echoed in Vatican Council II's image of the Church as "People of God." It is a beautiful, challenging ideal for which adequate structures are only gradually emerging: parish councils, diocesan boards, due process, personnel boards, broad consultation, increased liturgical participation of all Catholics.

Almost every parish experiences the tension created by so dramatic a change of the Church's self-understanding. Community does not just happen. People do not easily assume responsibilities formerly reserved to the clergy. Tolerance of differences while preserving unity rests on mutual respect, skillful listening, genuine sharing, and efforts at mutual understanding. New structures do not easily replace old ones. But whatever the practical difficulties, the Church today—as in its earliest days—sees itself first and foremost as a communion of people, united in a common faith in Jesus Christ.

What ultimately creates and holds together so human a fellowship is the Holy Spirit. Centuries ago, St.

Irenaeus wrote: "Where the Spirit of God is, there is the Church and every grace." A spiritual dynamic, much more than legislative authority or ecclesiastical ties, or psychological techniques—important as all these are—is at the heart of the Church's unity. The Church is primarily a spiritual union. Spirituality is more vital than structural renewal. The Church lives and grows through the Spirit of Christ, the Holy Spirit, who breathes where He will.

As a spiritual community, the Church escapes simple, clear ecclesiastical definition. While being a visible, organized institution, it is not neatly limited to those who are identified as Roman Catholics. The Council clearly recognizes evidence of the existence of God's People outside the institutional boundaries of Roman Catholicism. Profoundly significant is the fact that the Council's document on the Church begins with a chapter on the Church as *mystery.*

As mystery, the Church always eludes overly confining definitions. It eludes quantitative measurement, philosophical theory, and sociological research. Insight into the Church is best approached as the Scriptures and Vatican Council II attempt, through the reverent, prayerful consideration of a variety of models or images: God's sheepfold, vineyard, temple, flock, city, bride, body or people. Wonder at the mysterious depth and breadth of the Church's Spirit-filled dimensions is more properly Christian than overly intellectual, scientific definition. Totally human, yet living by the Spirit, the Church as God's People remains a profound mystery to be entered into with reverence and wonder.

Church as a Pilgrim People

Such an attitude creates a more modest, open mentality regarding the Church. Seeing the Church chiefly as a community of people suggests *how human a reality it is* in fact. No matter how spiritual its source in God's Spirit, it remains a fellowship of human beings. It may seem a Church of saints at times, at others it is patently a Church of sinners. Normally it appears as a blend of both. Even a superficial acquaintance reveals that the Church does not possess all the answers to life's complex questions. Likewise, it is evident that it does not possess everything people need to be saved, or freed, in this life and the next. Basic essentials of spiritual wisdom and sacramental helps, by all means; but everything, hardly.

So the Church today understands itself, as the Council movingly records, as a "pilgrim Church," a "pilgrim People." (*Church,* 8). Like every other group of human beings, the Church wanders through life's ambiguities, seeking a safe path to its final goal. The Church shares the common search of all people, a wayfarer, or fellow traveller, along with everyone else. It is a "Pilgrim People," proud of its riches of grace and knowledge, but aware of its need to learn from others. Along the way of life, the Church learns as well as teaches, receives as well as sheds light, receives healing as well as heals others.

The image of the Church as people on pilgrimage is a dramatic change in the Church's self-understanding in our time. Most of us grew up in a very self-assured Church. We were to teach the world, to convert those of false religions to the Roman Catholic Church. We may have heard that "outside the Church there is no salvation." For us, the Church was a secure rock amidst the erroneous, harmful winds of the world. It was a stable ship tossed about but uninfluenced by the world's treacherous waves.

Now we are called pilgrims finding our way hand in hand with other wayfarers. Without renouncing its mission to teach and heal, the Church recognizes that, like everyone else, it needs to learn and be healed. The rolling circle seems more apt than the stolid pyramid. The Church develops, grows, and learns in dialogue and collaboration with others who also seek life and light such as: fellow Christians and those of other religious traditions, particularly the Jews, persons dedicated to the cause of truth and justice, scientists, artists, social and political leaders, even though they be agnostics or atheists (see, for example, *Church in World,* 40-45). On its pilgrimage, the wayfaring Church needs to look for signs of God's presence and word everywhere, in the "signs of the times" and the "voices of our age," in contemporary values, profound experiences and questions, troubling issues, world developments and crises, and the daily joys, anxieties and frustrations we share with everyone else (*Church in World,* 1-4, 11, 44).

So the Church moves on its way, learning with others in a joint quest. Rooted in Christ, illumined by His Word, sustained and guided by the Spirit, to be sure but still on the way, always needing reform and renewal. Ordinary people, bonded by a common faith enriched by personal and cultural differences, we share Christ's riches from our own tradition while discovering Him in unsuspected "secular" sources.

Pope Paul sums it all up in words spoken as he opened the second session of the Council: *"The Church is a mystery. It is a reality imbued with the hidden presence of God. It lies, therefore, within the very nature of the Church to be always open to new and greater exploration."*

Church: Circle or Pyramid?

Ideas like these, at least in germ, surfaced during that evening of sharing as we sat together in a circle instead of facing a speaker's podium in silence. It was frustrating—we were so unaccustomed to such sharing, so unskilled at listening, so short on honest respect, so lacking in practice at real understanding of another. But it was exciting and enriching. We were amazed at the richness of experience and insight that was shared, at how people's differing gifts complemented one another, at how close we were becoming despite the vehement expression of deeply felt differences. We tried to listen and understand. We shared out of our own lives. We grew in an experienced awareness that, while the Church remains a world-wide institution, it is most of all ordinary people who share a faith in Jesus Christ and His Father, who have some experience of Their Spirit, and who recognize their need to share together in a common search. We left with a clearer awareness that the Church is a "People," humanly diverse for all its unity in the Spirit, very needy in spite of its spiritual riches, a mystery to be entered into and explored, as we share with all people the common earthly pilgrimage.

SUGGESTED ACTIVITIES

Primary Level

1. *Read a Child's Book:* To help the children sense the community dimension of Church, read to them the delightful book, *Swimmy,* by Leo Lionni (New York: Pantheon, 1963). Or show them the film version (Connecticut Films, Inc., 6 Cobble Hill Rd., Westport, CT 06880).

Guide them in talking about the story and their feelings about it. Help them see themselves like little fish in the larger group of fishes making up a large fish. Help them see Jesus as the central or most important fish. Point out that with Him, all the fishes make up one large fish.

If time allows, engage them in a simple creative activity. For example, give them (or have them make) smaller paper fish. Have them draw themselves or write their names on their fish. Do your own, and one of Jesus. Help them pin their fish to a board so as to make a large fish.

2. *Tell Gospel Stories:* Help the children realize that the Church is made up of people who know and love Jesus Christ, and that Jesus is with us always. Tell them one or two stories from the Gospels, stories that reveal Jesus' love for people and their trust in Him. The story of Zacchaeus might be most appropriate (Luke 19:1-10). Tell it in your own words. Or use a child's version like *Zacchaeus* (Minneapolis: Augsburg Press, 1970). Or a sung version like "Zacchaeus," on the album *Jesus Lives* from the Silver Burdett Religious Education Program (Morristown, N.J.: Silver Burdett, 1977). Guide them in talking about their own 'knowledge and love of Jesus.

Intermediate Level

1. *Show a filmstrip:* Carefully select and preview an appropriate filmstrip. One you might find useful is *"A Community People,"* part of the filmstrip series, *A Sacrament People* (ROA Films, 1696 N. Astor St., Milwaukee, Wi. 53202).

Show it to the students. Give them a few moments to think about it. Then guide them in discussing their reactions to it. Help them focus particularly on features that bring out the community nature of the Church, our spiritual bond with Christ, and our constant need to grow and learn.

2. *Study a Gospel Story:* Have the youngsters read carefully the beautiful story of Jesus breakfasting with the disciples on the seashore (John 21:1-14—but particularly 9-14). Then have them draw or paint the scene, being sure to include Jesus, the disciples, the charcoal fire with bread and fish cooking—or Jesus serving bread and fish to the disciples sitting around the fire.

Let them display and talk about their work. Guide them to see that the story and their pictures really portray what the Church is—a community of Jesus' friends, united because of Him, finding in Him their nourishment and strength. Point out that the fish was an early symbol of Jesus, and that bread continues to be a symbol of Him in the Eucharist.

Secondary Level

1. *Discuss:* With small groups of about four to six people, suggest some of the following questions for discussion: *How do you feel about the Church as a "pilgrim people"? What obstacles do you see to translating this model of the Church into practice? Why? What personal challenges and fears does it create in you to view the Church as people in pilgrim-*

age? What is your favorite image of the Church? Why?
After at least 20 minutes of discussion, have the
groups compare the resulting new insights with their
reaction to your presentation of this model. Encourage
questions from them.

2. *Study Images:* Each person or small working team
will need a copy of *The Documents of Vatican II* and
the *Bible.* Have them read in the *Dogmatic Constitution
on the Church,* chapter 2, "The Mystery of the Church."
Ask them to list the images of the Church that are used
to probe the mystery of the Church, e.g., sheepfold,
land or vineyard, building or temple, mother or spouse,
body, people, pilgrim people.
   Each person or team then takes one of the images,
draws it on newsprint or an overhead transparency.
Then the biblical references found in the Vatican II text
with each image may be looked up and discussed.
Words can then be added to the drawn image to bring
out the main dimension of the Church's reality expressed and highlighted by that image. Then all the images should be shared and displayed for further discussion.

3. *Do Autobiographical Sketch:* Alone or with your
group reflect on how your own faith has grown over the
years and what have been the major influences on its
growth. Then write a brief "Autobiography of My Faith"
or "The Story of My Faith."
   Afterwards, note and compare with others the impact
of *people* and *experiences* in your life that have affected your growth in faith. Discuss your findings.

4. *Meditate:* Help create a quiet atmosphere for meditation. Suggest that the group read silently, or have
someone read aloud one or more of the biblical passages relating to the pilgrim people image. After time
for meditation, invite spontaneous prayer. End with appropriate song or hymn.

Adult Level

1. *Rearrange Room:* If you feel secure and skilled enough in a non-directive, questioning approach, try what is described in the beginning of the chapter. Have the room arranged with chairs in orderly rows facing a podium, lectern or desk. Challenge the group to explore what the arrangement of the room might suggest about the nature of religious education and the Church. Gently challenge them with questions, reflecting back their own feelings and ideas, without giving your own interpretations. When you sense the proper moment, invite them to rearrange the room and consider what the new arrangement suggests about the Church.

2. *React to Book:* Read to the group Shel Silverstein's profound but simple book, *The Missing Piece* (Harper & Row, 1700 Montgomery St., San Francisco, Ca. 94111). Perhaps read it a second time. Encourage the group to share their reactions to the story, what it says to them.

Then, when they have more deeply analyzed and appreciated the story, ask them what the story might suggest about the Church as a pilgrim people. Challenge them to explore honestly their ideas and feelings about the Church from the perspective of *The Missing Piece.*

3. *Share Questions:* Take some time now to think of the questions you have about life, God, the Church, etc. Write down questions that really interest or trouble you. In teams, share the questions you all have, making a common list of the questions most often mentioned. Share these with the whole group and a master list compiled of common questions. The questions could be pursued over the next months in order of priority.

4. *Analyze parish/diocese:* After the group has carefully reflected on the meaning of pilgrim people, invite

them to examine their own parish and/or diocese in relation to the ideas in the article. Suggest that they list every positive sign or indication of their parish or diocese becoming more consciously a "people," a "pilgrim people." It is vital that the main emphasis be on the positive. Then more negative aspects of an honest critique can be examined within a more wholesome, creative, challenging mentality. To be avoided is simply a gripe session approach.

RESOURCES

"A Community People," part of *A Sacrament People.* Color filmstrip, record or cassette, teacher guide (ROA Films, 1696 N. Astor St., Milwaukee, Wi. 53202).

Swimmy. A six-minute, 16 mm. film adaptation of the marvellous book about "community" by Leo Lionni (Connecticut Films, Inc., 6 Cobble Hill Rd., Westport, Ct. 06880).

The Traveller (ROA Films, 1696 N. Astor St., Milwaukee, Wi. 53202). Color filmstrips trace the history of the Church down through the centuries.

READINGS

Avery Dulles, S.J., *Models of the Church* (Doubleday, Garden City, N.Y., 11531). Chapters 1, 3, and 7 relate to the theme of the article.

Recent catechisms briefly consider the history of the Church and the Church as pilgrim people or mysterious communion, for example: *A New Catechism: Catholic Faith for Adults* (Seabury Press, 815 Second Ave., N.Y., N.Y. 10017), pp. 135-144, 193-235; *A Common Catechism* (Seabury Press, pp. 322-346; *The Teaching of Christ: A Catholic Catechism for Adults* (Our Sunday Visitor, Huntington, Ind. 46750), pp. 186-200; Andrew M. Greeley, *The Great Mysteries* (Seabury Press, 815 Second Avenue, New York, N.Y. 10017).

Andrew M. Greeley, *The Communal Catholic* (Seabury Press). A personal and controversial manifesto on the emergence of the "communal" as opposed to the "ecclesial" Catholic in the United States.

Paul Hinnebusch, O.P., *Community in the Lord* (Ave Maria Press, Notre Dame, Ind. 46556); Max Delepesse, *The Church Community: Leaven and Lifestyle* (Ave Maria Press). Both offer contemporary interpretations of the Church as community.

Shel Silverstein, *The Missing Piece* (Harper & Row, 105 East 53rd St., New York, N.Y. 10022).

"I want those you have given me to be with me where I am."

John 17:24

Carl Pfeifer

3

The Church as an Institution

I recently saw a beautiful stained glass window that sparked nostalgic thoughts and feelings about the Church. The window showed, in deep blues and reds, a solidly constructed ship, buffeted by waves, sailing securely through the stormy sea. A Latin caption read: "Let us sail to a secure port." The ship obviously symbolized the Church, the "bark of Peter," sailing safely through life's hazardous waters.

As I gazed at the sturdy ship, I was reminded of another image that conveyed the same kinds of awesome feelings. G. K. Chesterton, in a famous passage, described the Church as a carriage careening over the rough, treacherous roads of history, veering this way and that to avoid danger, frequently on the verge of falling over or apart, but somehow coming through the dust of each crisis right-side-up and in one piece.

Both symbols convey a sense of wonder at the Church's ability to experience, endure and survive so much for so long. They suggest in picture the admiration of the ecclesial institution which the British historian Macaulay gave expression to in words that have become classic.

"There is not and there never was on this earth, a work of human policy so well deserving of examination as the Roman Catholic Church . . . No other institution is left standing which carries the mind back to the times when the smoke of sacrifice rose from the Pantheon, and when camelopards and tigers bounded in the Flavian amphitheatre. The proudest royal houses are but of yesterday, when compared with the line of the Supreme Pontiffs. That line we trace back in an unbroken series, from the Pope who crowned Napoleon in the nineteenth century to the Pope who crowned Pepin in the eighth, and far beyond the time of Pepin the august dynasty extends, till it is lost in the twilight of fable."

Macaulay's impressive prose captures something of the sense of pride Catholics have a right to have in their Church. It has a remarkable history. The Catholic Church has survived persecutions from without and subversion from within, cataclysmic cultural changes, political turmoil and wars, plagues and natural disasters, internal strife, corruption, incompetence and laxity, as well as the ordinary ills that all humans experience—and this for some 20 centuries in the most diverse corners of the globe.

Not only has the Church survived, but it has had a massive impact for good. Without the Roman Catholic Church, the entire Western world would be immeasurably impoverished. Much of what we take for granted today in areas of art, science, literature, music, architecture, history, medicine, law, politics and social services has been significantly influenced by the Church.

For more than 200 decades, the Church has helped millions of men and women discover reasons for living and reasons for dying. Jesus Christ and His saving message have found a place in the minds and hearts of persons of every station in life in every part of the world through the faithful preaching of the Gospel by the Church. The Church has inspired saints and called sinners back to God, encouraged the weak and motivated the strong, and aided great and small in grappling hopefully with life's fearful challenges. Ancient catacombs, medieval cathedrals, modern churches, missionary chapels dot the globe giving silent witness to the enduring spiritual contribution of the Church.

Pride in the Church's goodness and creative contributions must be balanced with humble admission of its immense power for evil and destruction. We dare not forget or deny such dreadful realities as the persecutions of the Jews, gross and subtle forms of anti-Semitism, the terrorism of the Crusades and Inquisition, the condemnation of creative people and the suppression of new ideas, the collaboration with colonialist injustices and identification with forces of oppression and exploitation, the self-righteous disdain for those of other faiths, the indifference to social injustices like prejudice and slavery.

The evils the Church must admit to are vast. So, too, are its positive contributions to the world at large as well as to its members. The magnitude of both sides of the Church's reality makes one intensely aware that the Roman Catholic Church—whatever its mystical depths and interpersonal bonds of community love—is a remarkable institution, enriched and encrusted with structures, rituals, and laws bearing the marks of some 200 decades of experience.

Excessive Institutionalism

Because it is so impressive an institution, with such great strengths and weaknesses, the Church runs the risk of being either overesteemed or undervalued. The latter is perhaps the contemporary trend, whereas the former dominated the climate in which most of today's Catholic adults grew up.

The modern history of the Church, from roughly 1550 to 1950, witnessed the excessive glorification of the Roman Catholic Church as an institution. Reacting to the charges of the Protestant Reformers, with their criticism of the hierarchy and their emphasis on the internal, spiritual experience of faith, Catholic theologians and catechists stressed the external, institutional aspects of the Church and public adherence to a clearly definable tradition. The rapid multiplication of reformation churches encouraged the felt need for clear, visible criteria for recognizing the "one, true Church" and its faithful members. To meet the challenge, the great Jesuit theologian and catechist, Robert Bellarmine, defined the true Church and its members exclusively in terms of such external, institutional criteria. His approach dominated Catholic catechesis and ecclesiology up into our own time.

Bellarmine's emphasis was on the Church as an institution like the other political societies of his time. He wrote that the Church is a society "as visible and palpable as the community of the Roman people, or the Kingdom of France, or the Republic of Venice." Using that socio-political model, theologians came to speak of the Church as a "perfect society," subordinate to no other institution, and like the state, possessing all the needed means of securing the happiness of its members. Emphasis focused more and more on the external, visible, legal dimensions of the Church as an institution. With this narrowed view of the Church as a visible, observable society or organization, the center of interest increasingly rested in the hierarchy and clergy, in laws and proper procedures, in the Church itself rather than in the world around it.

Catechisms translated the institutional model of the Church into simpler language, but did little to modify or balance it. As a result, the predominant image of the Roman Catholic Church in popular belief as well as in ecclesiastical documents and theological treatises was that of a vast institution, organized much like the monarchical states of Europe, structured like a pyramid, with the really important members at the top. A typical seminary course on the Church as late as the early 1960's might have roughly 40 "theses" or chapters, of which some 35 would deal with the hierarchy, the primacy of the pope, papal infallibility, and similar clerical, institutional concerns.

Even today, it is not unusual to hear many Catholics use the word "Church" in reference to the clergy and hierarchy.

Vatican Council II Corrective

Such an overly institutional model of the Church was even presented to the Bishops at the Second Vatican Council. Bishop Emile De Smedt of Bruges dramatically stood up before his fellow Bishops and radically rejected the proposed draft on the Church. He contended that such an institutionalized model of the Church was marred by excessive (1) clericalism, (2) juridicism, and (3) triumphalism. He criticized the pyramid model of the Church in which all authority, teaching and healing came from above, namely from the pope, bishops and priests. He also challenged the validity of defining the Church primarily by way of analogy with secular states.

Other Bishops rose up to voice similar objections. As a result, the original draft was rejected. The eventual *Constitution on the Church* reveals a radical shift in emphasis back to models of the Church that are far more traditional and balanced. The very first chapter of the Council's document gives the key. It is about "The Mystery of the Church." Its language and center of interest is the New Testament awareness of the Church as a profound mystery, grounded in the experience of the Risen Lord and His Spirit. The spiritual reality of the Church is seen as primary. As Bishop Ignatius of Antioch wrote in about 115 A.D.: "Where Jesus Christ is, there is the Catholic Church."

Since the presence of Jesus may be experienced by everyone, the Council considers "The People of God" in the *Constitution's* second Chapter. Only after considering the whole Church, embracing all who receive the Spirit of Jesus, does the Council address, in Chapter Three, the institutional aspects of hierarchy, laity, clergy, and religious.

The Vatican Council II teaching is a major corrective to the overly institutionalized image of the Church common for the past four centuries. By the time of the Council, it has become clear that the excessive institutional claims of the post-reformation model of the Church were in many instances historically indefensible and theologically unfounded in the New Testament and the soundest tradition of the Church. The institutionist model had grown up in the Counter-Reformation, and to some extent earlier in the late Middle Ages, prompted to a large extent by attacks on the hierarchical structure of the Church. As in most heated debates, a defensive effort at refutation tended to over-emphasize the points being attacked. In the calmer climate of Vatican II, a more balanced portrait of the Church could emerge which highlights its spiritual, mysterious and community aspects, without denying its institutional realities.

Backlash

The corrective of Vatican Council II has had many tangible effects on Catholic experience as well as catechesis and theology. A new sense of being "real" members of the Church has been experienced by many lay men and women who previously considered only clergy and religious as Catholics in the fullest sense. A renewed interest in spiritual experience and prayer seems to be widespread, uniting lay persons, priests, religious and sometimes bishops in a shared spiritual search. Lay persons are now visible and active in the celebration of the Eucharist in roles formerly reserved for the clergy. A sense of the Church as "community" more than as "institution" is felt by young and old in parishes around the country. Charismatic experience of the Spirit has revitalized families and parishes. In some parishes, dedicated and competent lay persons are looked to more than the clergy for insights into Scripture, spirituality, theology. Ecumenical sharing occurs on lofty theological levels and in shared collaboration on the parish level. There is significantly less evidence of a uniform, monolithic or pyramidal Church structure.

Basically all this is good and in accord with the Church's own present self-understanding of itself as God's people united with Him and with one another in Jesus Christ through the action of the Holy Spirit. But the experience of spiritual, personal and community renewal, combined with the anti-institutional milieu in which we all live, may be having some potentially harmful reactions. It is no secret that more and more good Catholics have less and less respect for their bishops and priests. The attitudes of good Catholics to institutional teachings about birth control, or institutional laws like Sunday Mass, or institutional customs like Saturday confession have changed dramatically in the last decade or so.

The risk of our time is the undervaluing of the institutional, organizational aspects of the Church. Catholics may underestimate, if not reject, the need and value of structure, as they recover traditional Catholic appreciation for the spiritual, mystical, charismatic dimensions of the Church. Love itself is of priceless value as the very life-blood of the Church, but love, to be effective even in a small community, requires some structures and procedures. Community is more important than institution, but institution can help express and preserve community.

It is very instructive to read the earliest history of the Church as recorded already in the New Testament. It all began with the enthusiastic experience of the Spirit of Jesus. Small groups of believers met informally in their homes to pray and "break bread" and hear the teachings of the Apostles. Charisms abounded. Spiritual experiences were commonplace. Community was intensely real.

Yet in this deeply spiritual climate, structures and rules soon emerged to protect and deepen the experienced spirituality. The Apostles quickly found a replacement for Judas, set up the order of deacons to serve the needs of the poor, legislated the requirements of membership, organized collections, settled disputes, sent out missionary teams and appointed leaders of local communities. The offices and procedures differed from place to place, but give evidence that the Spirit-filled communities were very quickly led by that Spirit to create necessary structures, rules, rituals and organized patterns of action.

Since those early experiences, the Catholic Church continually adapted its institutional forms to changing times. Democratic forces influence Church structures today, just as monarchical forces once exerted influence, as did imperial forces even earlier. The institutional forms of the Church will always be affected by the political institutions of the world in which it exists. But whatever the fluctuations in form, the Church will always remain an institution, for the simple sociological fact that communities of people require structure just as the body needs a skeletal structure. To reject the Church as institution is as unbalanced as to make institution the dominant aspect of the Church. There will always be a tension between community and institution, spirit and structure, freedom and law, authority and charism, mystery and the need for definition. But both remain necessary—even in the Church.

For a long time, we were so taken with the awesome "bark of Peter," the careening carriage of Chesterton, that we tended to lose sight of the people they contained or the Spirit Who guided them. Now that we have happily rediscovered the people and the Spirit, it would be sad to overlook the ship or carriage in which they still need to ride.

SUGGESTED ACTIVITIES

Primary Level

1. *Study Shepherds:* Show the children several photos of shepherds with their sheep. Draw from them their ideas and feelings about the work of the shepherd— how the shepherd feels about his sheep, how the sheep feel about the shepherd, what the sheep need from the shepherd, what he does for them, etc.

Then share with them the biblical image of Jesus as Good Shepherd. Simplify, for example, John 10:11-16. Probe the biblical image in terms of what they came to know about shepherds.

Finally show them a picture of their bishop. Remind them that the bishop's staff was originally a shepherd's staff. Help them grasp that the bishop is the "shepherd" of the local church. He is aided by the parish priests in his "shepherding" role of service to the community.

2. *Introduce parish priests:* Invite one or more of the parish priests to visit with you and the children. Ask them to tell the children about their work in the parish. Encourage the children to ask questions of the priests. After sufficient talking, all might share cookies and milk.

3. *Learn about Hierarchy:* Arrange photos of the pope, of the local bishop, other bishops, the local parish priest, and other priests, and deacons. Help the children identify each person pictured. Fill in for them any interesting facts you may know about these leaders and their work.

Intermediate Level

1. *Study Bible Passages:* Guide the youngsters in a

study of one or more of the following passages from the Acts of the Apostles: Selection of Matthias, 1:15-25; Need of Assistants, 6:1-7. Help them recognize that the earliest communities of Christians found it desirable and necessary to select and commission individuals to certain offices within the community.

Then help youngsters examine the Church today to discern the various offices (papal, episcopal, sacerdotal, deaconal) that developed over the centuries within the growing, changing church community.

Help them become more familiar with the role of the hierarchy. Guide them in exploring the value of and difficulty of such institutionalized offices in the Church community.

2. *Learn Traditional Creeds:* The *Apostles' Creed* and the *Nicene Creed* (Prayed at Sunday Mass) are ancient expressions of essential Catholic beliefs. They are in most missals and in most catechetical textbooks or catechisms. Duplicate them for the children if they do not have copies handy. Then encourage them to compare the two ancient creeds. They might note down similarities and differences. Encourage memorization of both creeds.

3. *Pray Litany of Saints:* Introduce the youngsters to the Litany of the Saints. Go through it to see if they recognize any of the names. Take time to talk about any of the saints in whom they seem interested. (The litany may be found in the missal as part of the Easter Vigil liturgy.)

Secondary Level

1. *Interview:* Before coming to the meeting, the teens are to interview five people about their understanding of the Church. The basic question would be, "How would you describe or define the Catholic Church?" Additional questions can be added by each inter-

viewer. The interviews are to be written up in summary form and brought to the meeting or class. (If possible, have them duplicated or copied so that all have copies of all the interview summaries.)

Divide the group into small working teams of 4 to 6 persons. Give them a set of interviews to work with. They are to read them and discuss them. Then they are to try to reduce all of them to one or two general statements that summarize at least the major thrust of the interviews. They should then evaluate the statements, noting anything important they seem to leave out, anything they stress too much, etc.

When the teams have finished their summaries and evaluations, they are to share their findings with the whole group. In this way, the whole group has a chance to share the findings of all, and to evaluate them. They might also attempt to come up with a final consensus statement describing the Church, based on all the work that has preceded.

2. *Evaluate the Institution:* Working in teams or in one large group, the class might try to create as large a list as they are able of things that impress them about the Church as an institution down through the ages as well as in today's world. Then challenge them to evaluate at least the more important of the events or realities listed. They could try to weigh the positive and negative contributions of the Church as they show it in their list. Help them notice what role the institutional aspects of the Church played in these positive and negative contributions. Invite them, in the light of their findings, to describe the institutional dimension of the Church.

3. *Pray Creed:* Lead the group in praying together the Apostles' Creed. After each phrase, pause for about 30 seconds to allow for quiet reflection on the words. For example, "I believe in God," pause, "the Father almighty," pause, "Creator of heaven and earth," pause,

etc. In this way, the prayer can become a kind of rhythmic meditation on the words of the prayer.

Adult Level

1. *Find images:* We've mentioned the image of a ship or that of a carriage as symbolic of the Church. Challenge the group to think back on their own experience, the churches they attended, the catechisms they used, stained glass images of the Church, images used in sermons, in order to recall any other images of the Church that were part of the Catholic culture in which they grew up. Guide them in discussing the implications of these images for their idea of the Church. If time permits, they might draw the symbols they remember before entering into discussion about them. Invite them to try to discover any significant changes in more recent images and symbols of the Church.

2. *Discuss:* After the adults have listened to your presentation, invite them to discuss it, in smaller teams or as a whole group, with these questions as a help.

3. *Evaluate Institutional Change:* The chapter cites a criticism of the pre-Vatican II Church as excessively (a) clerical, (b) legalistic, and (c) triumphalistic. In small groups or all together, list continuing evidence of these three symptoms in the Church today. Then draw up a list of indications of a shift away from these symptoms.

Compare and interpret together the results of the list making. Guide the group in evaluating the developments they noted and in exploring ways the trends away from these institutionalist ills might be furthered.

RESOURCES

The popular song, "Tradition," from *Fiddler on the Roof* celebrates the importance of a community's heritage (Columbia records, SX 30742).

The historical developments of the Church and its contributions to the world are presented as a personal narrative in the 10-filmstrip series, *The Traveller* (ROA Films, 1696 N. Astor Street, Milwaukee, Wisc. 53202).

READINGS

Avery Dulles describes the institutional model of the Church on pages 31-42 of his *Models of the Church* (Garden City, N.Y. 11531: Doubleday, 1974).

George Devine presents a balanced view of the Catholic Church today and in the past in his book, *A Case for Roman Catholicism* (Morristown, N.J.: Silver Burdett, 1978).

A Pope for All Christians is an anthology of theological writings concerning the future role of the papacy in the Christian Church. Seven theologians from leading U.S. Christian denominations, including Jesuit Father Avery Dulles, write frankly about the problems and possibilities of an ecumenical papacy. (Paulist Press, 545 Island Rd., Ramsey, N.J. 07446).

Carl Pfeifer

4

The Church as Sacrament

"They have something we just don't have," admitted Joan. "Their care for one another, and for outsiders, is so evident. Being with them has changed my daughter. I've gone to some of their services myself. There is such a sense of peace and joy. Their spirit comes through in the way they care about one another. They will help anyone in need. I must say I'm impressed."

Joan, middle aged mother of a 20-year old daughter, was telling several friends about a local Christian community that her daughter had joined after a very mixed-up year. The young woman seemed to have put her life together through her involvement with this group.

I was impressed with the sincere admiration these mature women showed for a group of young adult Christians with whom they had become acquainted. They had nothing but praise for these young people. They mentioned how no one in the group was ever really in need. Doctors in the group treated their fellow group members free of charge. Anyone with a problem found support and guidance from the group. Finances were shared where necessary. There was strong leadership and obvious order, but apparently no authoritarianism or fear. Over and over, Joan and her mother mentioned the group's contagious, attractive love, peace and joy.

Their enthusiastic account reminded me of the descriptions in the Acts of the Apostles of the earliest Christian communities in Jerusalem (Acts 2:42-47; 4:32-37; 5:12-16). These communities attracted people because they were so evidently caring and close. Within a century, similar communities of Christians were found in Africa. Of them, history records the reaction of their astonished neighbors, who stopped on the streets to observe and comment: "Notice how they love one another!"

The young communities of Christians throughout the ancient Roman Empire attracted thousands of their fellow citizens to join them because their style of life revealed an inner spirit rarely seen elsewhere. People noticed that the Christians possessed something they themselves were unable to find, something they very much wanted to share.

So, too, with Joan and her daughter. They recognized that the daughter's community of young Christians had something they themselves lacked, in spite of their own personal Christian faith.

Listening to them talk about how they could "feel the presence of Jesus" through the group's actions and style of being together helped me realize better what is meant when the Vatican Council II and theologians speak of the Church as a "sacrament." For example, the Council's *Constitution on the Church* calls the Church "a kind of sacrament or sign of intimate union with God, and of the unity of all mankind" (1). The same document later refers to the Church as the "visible sacrament of saving unity" (9) and the "universal sacrament of salvation" (48). Other council documents speak of the Church as the "sacrament of unity" (*Liturgy*, 26) and "sacrament of salvation" (*Missions*, 42).

In describing the Church as "sacrament," the council is renewing an ancient tradition. Already in the early centuries of Christian history, great theologians like Cyprian and Augustine spoke of the Church as "sacrament." So, too, did St. Thomas Aquinas in the Middle Ages. In modern times, there has been a return to this ancient model of understanding the Church.

What the sacramental model suggests is the dynamic and intrinsic bond between the inner experience of

Christ in personal faith and communal love and the external expressions of faith and love in life-style, ritual, structure, organization, procedures, laws and actions. The experience of the Risen Lord—a personal spiritual experience—unites those with similar faith experience. This spiritual communion with Jesus and with one another in turn seeks expression in adequate organizational, ritual, and legal forms. These external forms are meant to reveal, protect, and deepen the shared spiritual experience.

The important relationship between spirit and structure is expressed by the word "sacrament." The Council of Trent beautifully defines a sacrament as "the visible form of invisible grace." The Second Vatican Council abbreviates the description of sacrament to "sign of grace." Both definitions sum up the traditional understanding of *sacrament as the visible, tangible shape of a present, but invisible spiritual reality*—namely the presence and activity of Jesus and His Spirit in the hearts of people.

The notion of sacrament involves both internal and external, invisible and visible, divine and human. Spiritual reality is expressed, deepened and communicated through the visible gestures and acts that make up the sacramental sign.

The understanding of sacrament is not unlike the understanding of the human body. Our bodies are the physical expression of our unique spirits or souls. The human spirit or soul is not a separate thing contained in the body, like water in a jar, or a prisoner in a jail. The body *is* the spirit or soul enfleshed. The spirit *is* the body enlivened. They are not two mutually distinct beings somehow glued or chained together. Body and spirit or soul are but two aspects of one reality, a human person.

So with sacrament. Christ's invisible, gracious presence in the community of believers finds expression in the visible, observable Church. In a mysterious manner, the Church *is* the "Body of Christ." It is at one and the same time "visible form" and "invisible grace," human institution and mystical communion.

Ideal and Challenge

The ancient and recent use of the sacrament model to describe the Church is an attempt to express the intimate relationship between the spiritual and institutional aspects of the Church. To describe the Church as sacrament is to sense something of the inner pull to bring spiritual experience and external structure into greater congruence. For many years, Catholics have been overly preoccupied with the institutional side of the Church. Recent trends sometimes so focus on the spiritual and mystical dimension of the Church as to neglect or reject its institutional or structural aspects. To see the Church as sacrament recognizes the reality of spiritual grace and visible form and the intimate bond between the two.

This may sound very abstract until one meets a Church whose organized life does reveal an inner spirit. Joan and her mother found such a Christian community in their hometown and observed its impact on the young people who were part of it. Jerusalem and Carthage, Athens, and Rome, witnessed and were converted by similar communities of Christians centuries ago.

In such cases, people's lives together give visible form to the invisible grace they experience. Just observing them gives one an impression of what human life might be at its best. By looking at a compelling example of a vital local church, people can catch a glimpse of how kind and thoughtful, how supportive and healing, how happy and creative people can actually be. Entering into the community may lead one to experience something of the peace and joy, the freedom and respect, the unity and love that men and women everywhere desire. In such communities of believers, Church tangibly becomes a "kind of sacrament or sign of intimate union with God, and of the unity of all mankind."

This sacramental model of the Church implies a tremendous challenge as well as a more satisfying intellectual understanding of the Church. It makes clear the ideal of Church, in which the community life-style and structures reflect the inner experience of the Spirit of Jesus. The external forms—of leadership, organization, procedure, law, ritual, worship, service—are meant to reflect the presence and guidance of the freeing, creative, healing, loving Spirit of the Risen Lord.

So understood, the Church clearly is always *becoming* the Church of Jesus Christ. At no time has or can the institutional Church, local or universal, give full and adequate expression to its inner relationship with Father, Son and Spirit. The Love that is at the core of the Church's being can never find total expression in any community of believers. There will always be a gap between the ideal and its realization. There will always be an inner tension, a constant groping to more closely approximate the ideal.

As the council so honestly states—again recapturing an ancient expression of Christian wisdom—the Church is constantly in need of renewal (*Ecumenism,* 6). As a *pilgrim people,* always on the way toward greater actuation of its giftedness, the Church needs constantly to reform and renew its spiritual and structural life. The criteria for such renewal are ultimately found in the life of Jesus, recorded in the New Testament and continually experienced by faithful Christians open to His Spirit. There is no room for ecclesial self-satisfaction or triumphalism.

One of the great values of viewing the *Church as sacrament* is a sense of spiritual and religious idealism, constantly at work to bring the expressions of community fellowship, worship, and service into greater conformity with the movements of the Holy Spirit. On-going development and renewal are recognized as a necessary, healthy part of attempting to realize more fully the ideal of Church. Such renewal cannot be merely more efficient management or organization, but must flow from the spiritual experience of the community. So, too, the renewal cannot remain simply spiritual or charismatic, without coming to grips with institutional or structural needs.

Viewing the Church not simply as "mystical communion" or primarily as "institution" but as "sacrament" also suggests the primacy of the symbolic over the statistical, of quality over quantity. There is a sense that the visible, tangible aspects of the Church are subject to quantitative, statistical analysis. Such statistics have their importance—for example, the growth or decline of members in the Church, the increase or decrease of confessions, the number of ordinations. But one genuine experience of Christian community, or sacramental reconciliation, or priestly concern may reveal more about the reality of Church than all the statistics. *The quality of life speaks more profoundly than the quantity of people or activities.*

What is most important, then, in Church renewal—or Church missionary or pastoral work—is the quality of Christian life experienced and evidenced by Christian communities. Who they *are,* what they *are,* how they *are* together is what gives moving evidence of and visible form to the invisible grace of Jesus Christ. It is not numbers of programs, numbers of sacramental celebrations, even numbers of converts that is of primary importance. What ultimately reveals the healing, saving, unifying presence of Jesus' Spirit in a local Church—or in the Church universal—is the quality of life that becomes evident in how the people live, pray, work together in a freeing, uniting, creative way.

Then the Church becomes a sacrament or sign that lets people see—in a world marred by greed, graft, hatred, war, and crime—what God has in mind for human beings. People can come to recognize that it is possible to live in harmony and freedom, to find peace and joy in mutual love and service, to experience

closeness with others and with a gracious God—
because they can experience this in a community of
Christians who make up the Church. Church as sacrament holds the key to unlocking the meaning and mystery of life, because it is the visible, historical extension
of the saving presence of Jesus Christ.

Church: City on a Mountaintop

It is within this symbolic or sacramental perspective
that the Old Testament speaks of Jerusalem. Jerusalem is the city in which God's presence is specially to
be found. That presence becomes visible, attractive in
the peace, joy, justice and compassion evident among
Jerusalem's citizens. Peoples of all nations look to
Jerusalem for instruction and guidance as to how to
live. Jerusalem becomes a light to the world (see Isaiah
2:2-5; 60:1-22).

Jesus takes up the same symbolism in speaking of
His followers. He is the Light illuminating life's mystery
(John 8:12). That light is to be radiated out to the world
through the lives of His friends:

"You are the light of the world. A city set on a hill
cannot be hidden. People do not light a lamp and then
put it under a bushel basket. They set it on a stand
where it gives light to all in the house. In the same way,
your light must shine before men so that they may see
goodness in your acts and give praise to your heavenly
Father" (Matthew 5:14-16).

That is the challenge to the Church which sees itself
as a sacrament or sign of Christ's unifying, saving,
enlightening presence. The inner Light must become
visible in the community's life-style. Then men and
women will look at the Church, as Joan and her mother
looked at her daughter's Christian community, and
remark, "They have something we just don't have."

SUGGESTED ACTIVITIES

Primary Level

1. *Explore Light:* Guide the children in a creative exploration of the symbolism of "light." Help them experience darkness and light. Show them slides of various kinds of light. Guide them in noting how light and darkness make them feel. Focus on light as illumination and as warmth, as a source of joyful, happy feelings and a dispeller of fear, sadness.

Then share with them Jesus' words about being the Light of the World—Jesus first and secondly, all who believe in Him (John 8:12; Matthew 5:14-16). Help them relate Jesus' words to their own experience by having them light individual candles from a central Christ-candle. Guide them in talking about how that light can shine in the lives of Christians.

2. *Learn a Song:* Teach the children a song that deals with the biblical theme of light. Or at least listen with them to a song about light. For example: "You Are the Light of the World," "Christ-Light," "I've Got a Light," "O Lord, Give Us Light," or "This Little Light of Mine." (See the RESOURCES list) Then guide them in talking about what the song says to them. Sing it, listen to it, as a prayer.

3. *Draw:* Read to the children the words of Jesus (Matthew 5:14) about a city set on a hill. Draw from them their understanding of what Jesus means. Help them interpret the words in relation to their experience.

Then suggest that they draw or paint what Jesus' words suggest to them. Have them display and talk about their completed work. Lead them in prayer that they, their Church, might become like such a city on a mountaintop.

Intermediate Level

1. *Invite Guest Speaker:* Invite a guest speaker to share with the youngsters personal experiences of church communities whose spirit is revealed in their attitudes and actions. There are many parishes, many specialized groups (e.g., Cursillo, Knights of Columbus, etc.), many religious communities which in their local community life, worship and service show forth the inner faith and love that motivate them. The recounted experiences should be as honest and factual as possible.

Encourage the youngsters to question and talk with the guest so that they get a clear idea and a positive feeling or attraction to the kind of Christian living that is described.

2. *Study New Testament:* Divide the group into three sub-groups. Have each group read one of the three passages in the Acts of the Apostles which describe the earliest Christian communities: (1) Acts 2:42-47; (2) Acts 4:32-37; (3) Acts 5:12-16.

Have them explore why these communities were so attractive to so many people, leading eventually to the conversion of thousands of their fellow citizens.

Share with them Tertullian's report on how the Romans summed up the lives of their Christian neighbors: "Look at how they love one another!"

Then guide the youngsters in relating what they learned with their experience of their local parish community.

Secondary Level

1. *Make Graffiti Wall:* Divide the whole group into three sections. An easy way to do this is through color-coded name tags picked up at entrance to the room. You will need equal numbers of red, blue and green

coded tags. At an appropriate time, invite all those with the same color tags to gather together.

Ask them all to think of what the Church means to them. The "red" group is then to describe the Church by means of a single *verb.* The "blue" group describes the Church by means of an individual *person.* The "brown" group does the same with a single *symbol* or *image.*

Each individual in each group may come up with his or her description and write or paint it graffiti style on a large sheet of wrapping paper, butcher paper or poster board previously attached to a wall.

Then encourage the group to study the completed graffiti wall. Let them do this leisurely.

Perhaps the three groups could go back to work and try to come to a consensus about the *one* verb, person, and symbol they feel best summarizes their view of the Church. These could then be superimposed in heavier print on the graffiti wall.

2. *Study Texts:* Have the group study more carefully the quotations in the chapter from the Bible and the *Documents of Vatican II.* Perhaps divide the large group into smaller sub-groups, each assigned one or more texts. Then have each small group report its conclusions to the whole group.

Finally, guide them in formulating a position paper regarding the *Church as Sacrament,* drawing from their own experience of the Church and their conclusions after studying the various quotations.

3. *Create Media Show:* After exploring with the group the ideas found in the chapter, challenge them to create a media presentation on the *Church as Sacrament.* It might be a simple collage, using photos and words from magazines, or a more complex slide-sound show, or a dramatic production, or any other form of expression appropriate to their resources.

Adult Level

1. *Create People Collage:* Since the sacrament model is clarified by reference to the body as physical expression of the inner spirit, a bodily activity would be most appropriate. For example: Invite the group to think for a moment or two about the question: "How would you describe the ideal Church?"

Then invite a volunteer to come to the front and express his or her idea of the ideal Church without words by assuming a bodily position that expresses the idea. The position and gestures will have to be such that they can be maintained for about five minutes.

Then invite a second person to come up. This person is to build on the first person's expression, extending it, correcting it, enriching it. He or she may also begin a whole new "sculpture."

Invite about six volunteers in all to complete, one after another, the developing image of the ideal Church. Encourage honesty and creativity. The communication must be solely through bodily position and gesture.

When the collage or sculpture—or several of them— is completed, dissolve it backwards. Ask the last person, "Why did you do what you did? What were you trying to express?" Then move to the second last, and so on down to the first volunteer. Allow each to clarify and interpret the meaning of the position taken.

Finally invite the whole group to comment and talk about the experience. Ask them to comment on the image or images of Church that emerged from the bodily sculptures and verbal clarifications. Ask if they feel anything important was missing from the whole collage, or if anything seemed overemphasized or undervalued. Encourage free and honest discussion. Some might prefer to make or complement their comments through bodily gesture.

2. *Evaluate Sacramentality:* After the group has studied and discussed the article, divide them into teams—"parish," "diocese," "nation," "world." Suggest that they think about the Church as they know it on their assigned level—parish, diocesan, national and universal or international.

Have them note down the external, visible, aspects of the Church as they or others may observe it. These can be listed, or drawn as a kind of composite portrait.

Then have them examine the external in terms of sacramental or sign value. For example, Sunday Mass is experienced as a very happy, friendly hour. What does that suggest about the nature of the Church? Or, the church is an imposing, expensive building in a depressed neighborhood. What does this suggest about the Church and its role in the world?

Encourage them to share and discuss their findings, guiding them to be more sensitive to the sacramental or sign dimension of the Church on all its levels from local parish to world-wide institution.

3. *Meditate/Pray:* Sing a hymn about the Church that suggests its sacramental nature. For example: "They'll Know We Are Christians by Our Love." Listen in silence as someone reads Jesus' words about our being the Light of the world, Matthew 5:13-16. Encourage several moments of silent meditation, aided perhaps by slides of lamps, candles, etc. Invite spontaneous prayers. End with a hymn expressing the theme of light.

READINGS

Avery Dulles, S.J., describes "The Church as Sacrament" in *Models of the Church* (New York: Doubleday, 1974) on pp. 58-70.

William J. Bausch offers a clear and practical explanation of the sacraments in *A New Look at the Sacraments* (Notre Dame. Ind., Fides/Claretian, 1977).

Charles J. Keating summarizes sacraments in *Christian Sacraments and Christian Growth* (W. Mystic, Ct., Twenty-Third Publications, 1977).

Bernard J. Cooke's series on the Sacraments can be found in Vol. 11 and Vol. 12 of *Religion Teacher's Journal,* W. Mystic, Ct. See also, his *magnum opus* on the Church and ministry, *Ministry to Word and Sacraments* (Philadelphia: Fortress Press, 1976).

RESOURCES

Father Richard Rohr, O.F.M., examines the theology of the Church against the background of Jesus, His life, teachings, and continued presence and activity. Six 90-minute cassettes explore *Jesus and His Church.* Available from St. Anthony Messenger Press, 1615 Republic Street, Cincinnati, Oh. 45210.

Christian Sacraments and Christian Growth (full-color filmstrip and record) offers new meaning to the personal renewal required of sacramental participation. (Twenty-Third Publications, P.O. Box 180, W. Mystic, Ct. 06388.)

A Sacrament People filmstrip series explores in various ways the sacramental dimension of the Church. (ROA Films, 1696 N. Astor St., Milwaukee, Wis. 53202.)

Songs: "You Are the Light of the World," *Godspell* (Stephen Swartz, New York: Bell Records, 1102, 1970); "Christ-Light," *Run, Come, See!* (Robert Blue, Chicago: F.E.L. Church Publications, S272, 1966.); "I've Got a Light," *I Love Life* (Sr. Roberta McGrath, Rocky Hill, CT: D & K Sound Services, DK9766, 1973); "O Lord, Give Us Light," *No Time Like the Present,* (Cincinnati: World Library of Sacred Music); "This Little Light of Mine," *Journey to Freedom* (Landon G. Dowdey, Chicago: Swallow Press, 1969).

Carl Pfeifer

5

The Church as Herald

A recent folklife festival I attended included an afternoon devoted to the rich American heritage of gospel music. One group of black singers was especially exciting. They were from a Baptist Church in the center of Washington's inner city. All ages seemed represented among the 80 or more members of the choir but I was struck with the large number of teenagers. The entire choir wore attractive green choir robes.

Their singing was fantastic, as was the live accompaniment by a small combo. A sense of joy became almost tangible as the gospel message resounded through their singing and rhythmic movements. You began to feel that what they sang about was really good news. Their spirit was contagious. The hundreds of spectators began to clap and sing along with the choir.

Then, when their performance was over, the green-clad singers fanned out into the crowd. They shook hands with people, spoke smilingly about Jesus and what He meant to them. A young woman, perhaps a high school senior, approached me. With genuine warmth and a bright smile, she invited me to come to their church any time. She said I was welcome to share with them the good news of Jesus. She obviously meant it. The message she sang so movingly with her fellow choristers seemed to be at home in her whole being.

I was touched by the experience. Often since, I have thought about how spontaneously the singers moved out among the spectators and confirmed in friendly words the joyful message of their gospel songs. They were eager to share with everyone in sight the good news that apparently meant so much to them. There was no pressure, no hardsell, just friendly sharing.

I could not help thinking they were doing what Jesus called His disciples to do—to share with others what they had themselves heard and experienced. Just as Jesus Himself went about telling everyone about His Father and the coming reign of God, He sent out His friends to do the same. In fact, His final instructions to the disciples were: "Go into the whole world and proclaim the good news to all creation" (Mark 16:15).

The New Testament records how extensively and convincingly Jesus' followers heralded the gospel message. It also reveals a consciousness on their part that such heralding or proclaiming was part of a Christian's self-identity. St. Paul, for example, speaks of himself and his fellow Christians as "ambassadors for Christ" (2 Cor 5:20). St. Peter urges the Christian communities already facing persecution to be ready to explain their hope gently and respectfully to anyone who questions them (1 Peter 3:15-16).

The experiences of those joy-filled gospel singers recalled to my consciousness this important aspect of my responsibility as a Christian. It also helped me sense an important dimension of the Church's identity and responsibility that has tended in recent years to become somewhat obscured. The Church as a whole, just as individual members, has the commission to go into the world as a herald or prophet of the Gospel. Prior to this, we have been taken up with models of the Church that focus more on its nature than its mission.

Those models tend to center on the internal make-up and workings of the Church. Even the sacrament model, while stressing that the Church is to be a sign to the world, focuses more on the congruence between inner spirit and outer forms. But to consider the Church as "herald" or "prophet" is to look more sharply at the Church's role and responsibility *to the world at large.* As a prophetic herald, the Church is to proclaim to the world—when convenient and when inconvenient (2 Timothy 4:2)—the Word of God, alerting people in all ages and places to the coming of the kingdom or reign of God.

The Second Vatican Council does not develop in much detail the model of Church as herald. But the Council consciously takes on that role. For example, the *Constitution on Revelation* begins by describing its task in terms of proclaiming the "message of salvation." The hoped for result of its heralding or kerygmatic effort is stated in the words of St. Augustine: "so that hearing the message of salvation the whole world may believe; by believing, it may hope; and by hoping, it may love" (Revelation 1).

The *Constitution on the Church in the Modern World* even more explicitly addresses itself to the world at large. The council sees itself as engaging with the world in conversation about important contemporary issues as well as basic questions of life's meaning, sharing with all mankind the "light kindled from the gospel" (*Church in World,* 3). This task is shared by the entire Church that is, the whole People of God. The Church is to proclaim Jesus Christ and the coming of God's kingdom—a kingdom of justice, peace, mercy and love.

Intimately involved in all that affects people in today's world, painfully aware of the apparent absence of God's kingdom in many aspects of a complex, changing world culture, the Church needs to remind people of the healing presence of a gracious God. The Church is to tell people over and over the most amazing news of all—that God loves us so much that He actually sent His Son to make possible a life of freedom, peace, mercy, joy, justice and love by entering fully into everything human and radically crippling the powers of evil. It is a message of hope, of the ultimate victory of good over evil, life over death, joy over sorrow, justice over injustice.

Herald of God's Kingdom

Such a message is credible only when people sense that the herald shares fully in the human condition while clinging to hope despite all evidence to the contrary. To be a credible prophet of God's kingdom, the Church, like Jesus, needs to become fully identified and involved with all humanity and deeply committed to the cause of justice and peace. The Church as herald needs to be marked by a sense of profound compassion and sensitive understanding. It is not called to judge and condemn as much as to warn, heal, forgive, and encourage. It may need to criticize at times, to take strong stands, to help people see the absence of God's kingdom in their lives—Jesus and all the prophets did that.

As herald, the Church points to *something* greater than itself—God's kingdom—to *someone* greater than itself—Jesus Christ, Who alone is Lord. It proclaims not its own words, but the Word of God. The Church is not the kingdom. The Church proclaims its coming and works to prepare people for its coming. It prays daily to God, "Thy kingdom come!" There is no room in a herald for self-righteousness or triumphalism. There is no place for any confusion between who is herald and who is Lord. Nor is there excuse for failure to proclaim the message because of fear or embarrassment.

Hearer of the Word

Jesus sketches a beautiful portrait of the Church as herald in His instructions to His newly chosen 12 apostles before sending them on their first missionary journey (Matthew 10:1-42). The entire instruction is worth reading, reminding us that the primary prerequisite for proclaiming the word and the kingdom is first to hear the word oneself and experience the kingdom in one's own heart.

Perhaps nothing is more critical to the *Church as herald* and to individual Christians as heralds than that they open themselves to hear God's saving Word. One of the more striking emphases of Vatican Council II is that placed on the importance of listening to God's Word. The Council documents repeatedly urge all Catholics to become more intimately familiar with the scriptures as they are understood within the Church's living tradition. Much of the liturgical revision of the Mass and other sacraments involved making the bible more important and intelligible in the revised rites. The bible was deliberately restored to a central place in Catholic life and worship.

The Council draws upon ancient Christian tradition in affirming that the bible deserves the same reverence as the eucharistic Body of Christ (*Revelation,* 21). This is a strong statement, suggesting that the Word of God is as important to the life of the Church as is the Eucharist. Since the Council, Catholics have become much more appreciative of the scriptures, but as yet few would probably consider listening to the biblical readings and homily at Sunday Mass as important as receiving communion.

Actually the Church is called into being, gathered together, sustained and sent back into the world by the Word of God. Without the ongoing hearing of the Word, there would be no Church. In a dramatic, poetic way the ancient Hebrew prophet, Hosea, suggests the vital role of God's Word in constituting God's People. Describing God as a lover, Hosea portrays Him as alluring His beloved, Israel, into the desert. There He speaks to her heart. His Word stirs in her a response of love, seals with her an undying covenant, making her His forever. His Word of love, "You are my people," calls forth her response, "My husband . . . my God" (Hosea 2:16-25).

So it continues to be. God's People, the Church, exists in response to God's loving, creative call. The original Greek word for Church in the New Testament, *ekklesia* means just that: "those who have been called out."

Jesus the Word

The New Testament develops this symbolism of the Hebrew scriptures. God's People is seen to be the Bride of Jesus Christ (*Revelation,* 21:1-4) and God's Word is recognized as Jesus (John 1:1-18). He continually calls her to closer union with Himself. In less poetic language, the Council stresses the same reality, teaching that Jesus "is present in His word, since it is He Himself who speaks when the holy Scriptures are read in the Church" (*Liturgy,* 7). So important to the life of the Church and the individual Christian is listening to the scriptures that St. Jerome, the ancient translator of the bible into Latin, wrote: "Ignorance of the scriptures is ignorance of Christ." The Council confirms Jerome's conviction (*Revelation,* 25).

Such awareness is at the root of the Church's renewed appreciation of the bible and of preaching. We Catholics have become more aware in recent years of the validity of the traditional Protestant valuing of the bible, just as many Protestant churches are recovering the traditional Roman Catholic regard for sacrament.

The *Church as herald* must listen to the very Word it proclaims. It does so by reading the scriptures and by interpreting them through preaching. But Vatican Council II also urges upon the Church and individual Christians the need to listen for God's Word in the world around it, in the "signs of the times," (*Church in World,* 4, 11), the "voices of our age," (*Church in World,* 44) and in those "seeds of the word" (*Missions,* 11) that are every expression of true value, of genuine goodness and beauty in the world. The herald must sensitively listen to the very people to whom He proclaims the gospel message, eager to recognize and confirm any evidence of God's Word already evident there. Again we find a healthy, humbling caution. As herald, the Church is sent to preach faithfully and fear-lessly God's Word and Kingdom, but it must ever be aware that it, too, is subject to that Word, who may speak to the herald from the most unsuspecting sources.

There is then a continual, creative tension within the Church between speaking and listening, proclaiming and hearing, preaching the kingdom and receiving it like a child (Luke 18:17). The very call to share with others the good news of Jesus Christ demands that one continually open one's mind and heart to the impli-cations of Jesus' gospel.

The Word of God is not simply a set of truths or doctrines. Much less is it a set of answers to all life's questions. God's Word is a person, Jesus Christ, who calls out to us to enter with Him more deeply into life's profoundest mystery—the cross that unlocks life, love, and joy. He calls his Heralds to walk with Him as friends as well as to go before Him as heralds.

I'm grateful to those green-robed gospel singers for bringing home to me forcibly yet gently the very real call I have to share with others the gifts I have received as a Christian. They helped me recognize more clearly the herald model for understanding the Church. They exemplified for me the words of John's first epistle which sums up the model of *Church as herald:*

"This is what we proclaim to you: what was from the beginning, what we have heard, what we have seen with our eyes, what we have looked upon and our hands have touched—we speak of the word of life. . . . What we have seen and heard we proclaim in turn to you so that you may share life with us. This fellowship of ours is with the Father, and with His Son, Jesus Christ. Indeed our purpose in writing you this is that our joy may be complete" (I John 1:1-4).

SUGGESTED ACTIVITIES

Primary Level

1. *Reverence the Bible:* Take a large Bible and reverently enthrone it in a special place—perhaps on a small pillow or a reading stand. Without saying anything, light one or more candles near the Bible. Then silently place incense before it. Kneel or bow profoundly in reverence. Then take the Bible, hold it up, and say "This is the Word of the Lord." Place it back reverently and bow or kneel before it once again.

Then ask the children what they know and feel about the Bible. Probe with them the significance of what you just did. Ask them if they have ever seen the Bible before, if they have ever seen it held up, or incensed. Ask them also if they have heard it read, and what they remember from it. In this way, help them appreciate the Bible as God's Word, to be honored and listened to with reverence, in private as well as in public worship.

2. *Dramatize Story of Samuel:* Study carefully beforehand the story of Samuel's call to a prophetic mission, as well as one or other example of his prophetic work: 1 Samuel 3:1-21 and perhaps 1 Samuel 7:2-6.

Tell or read from the Bible the story of Samuel's call. Guide them in sharing their reactions to the story. Help them note how it was actually God Who called him to do a special work, how it was only gradually and with Eli's help that Samuel discerned God's call.

Guide them in working out a simple dramatization of the story. Help them create simple stage effects and props. Allow them to play out one or more versions of the story.

Then talk with them about what the story says to them, and what it suggests about God's call in their lives and how important it is to listen for and to God's Word.

Intermediate Level

1. *Study a prophet:* Guide the youngsters in becoming acquainted with one or more of the great Hebrew prophets: Isaiah, Jeremiah, Ezekiel, Amos, Hosea, etc. Provide them with art works depicting the prophet and his teachings. Refer them to brief, selected biblical texts that help give a clue to the personality and message of the prophet.

Have them prepare, perhaps best in small groups, a display or bulletin board or similar presentation, which sums up what they have learned about the life and message of the prophet under consideration.

A helpful example of this type of biblical study may be found in the study of Jeremiah in *Growth in Spirit,* the sixth grade text of the Silver Burdett Religious Education Program by Janaan Manternach and Carl J. Pfeifer.

2. *Examine Bible texts:* Have the youngsters look up the various bible passages referred to in the chapter. It might help if you would copy out the references and print them neatly for the youngsters to see them.

Have them study each passage, trying to make sense out of it. Then encourage them to try to grasp what the passage might have to say to Christians today.

Suggest that they sum up their thoughts on how the Christian community today can hear God's word and then share it with others. Have them memorize one or other brief text from the Bible that relates to their summation.

3. *Learn about Modern Prophets:* Provide the youngsters with information on contemporary Christian heralds or prophets, or examples of the Church taking prophetic stands. Significant stands by the whole Church or by local churches on moral or social issues should also be included. Initiate them into reading the

diocesan newspaper for information and resources.

Help the youngsters explore the examples you select. Have them share what they discover. Guide them to deepen their appreciation of the Church's task of listening to God's Word and then sharing it with others.

Secondary Level

1. *Respond to Photos:* An interesting way to explore the relation between the Bible and daily life is through photographs. Many variations of the following two approaches may be worked out.

   a. Begin with a biblical text, preferably a brief one of just a few lines. Then search for one or more photographs (in magazines, newspapers, etc.) that illustrate the biblical quote. The photo might then be mounted on cardboard and the biblical text written below it in the form of a caption.

   b. Begin with photographs. They may be symbolic or realistic, or a mixture of the two. Search for the most appropriate biblical text you can find to interpret the photo. Then mount the two.

After the photos and biblical texts have been found, they may be shared and discussed by all, preferably in small teams who then report to the whole group. The discussion should focus on the relation of the Bible to significant life experiences.

A display of the photos and their biblical captions could be created and displayed in church or school so that the entire parish might share it.

2. *Study Sacred Art:* Jesus spoke and acted like a prophet. The Gospels provide many stories that reveal Jesus' prophetic role, and Christian artists down through the centuries have interpreted in various art forms the Gospel stories. Carefully select a series of art works that show Jesus teaching, preaching, healing, challenging the scribes and pharisees, cleansing

the Temple, etc. (Libraries, museums, churches, schools, art books are good sources of such art.) Display the art. Let the group study the various works and talk about them. Invite them to find the Gospel stories being depicted in the art. From the art and the Gospel stories, challenge them to come up with a brief written sketch or portrait of Jesus as Prophet. Then help them explore how this applies to the Church's role as *herald* or *prophet.*

3. *Meditate/Pray:* Several biblical texts on God's word can provide fruitful material for an extended period of prayer and meditation. For example, among many others you may also wish to use: *2 Timothy 3:15-17:* roles of scripture in Christian life. *Romans 15:1-6:* roles of scripture in Christian life. Read the texts in silence. Then have them read aloud. More silence. Follow the silent meditation with sharing of reflections. Close with spontaneous prayer and a hymn.

Adult Level

1. *Study Bible:* The role of the "prophet" or "herald" of God is dramatically described in both Old and New Testaments. In order to deepen your appreciation for the Church's prophetic role, it may be helpful to read and discuss several biblical texts.

Divide into small working teams—three or four persons per group at most. Each team will need at least one Bible. The following biblical passages could be divided up, one or two to each team. After the teams have studied and discussed their texts, they should share their conclusions with the entire group.

These texts are typical of many texts in the scriptures that suggest the prophetic role of individuals and of God's People as a whole: *2 Samuel 12:1-14:* Prophet Nathan challenges King David for his sins of murder and adultery. *Exodus 3:1-12:* Moses is called and sent by God to confront Pharaoh. *Jeremiah 1:4-10:* Jeremiah is called and sent by God to speak God's word to the nations and to Israel. *Ezekiel 2:1-10; 3:1-15:* Ezekiel is sent by God to confront Israel. *Joel 2:12-17:* Joel's prophetic call to God's people to repent. *Amos 5:7-15; 8:4-8:* Amos condemns Israel's injustice toward the poor. *Matthew 23:1-39:* Jesus confronts the religious leaders of his time.

Questions like the following might be used as guides in discussing the biblical texts: In whose name does the prophet speak? What is the prophet's message? To what extent is the message still valid? What does the text suggest about the Church's role as prophet or herald in today's world? What does it suggest about the individual's prophetic role?

2. *Analyze News Media:* Divide the class into working teams. Provide each team with a stack of recent newspapers, both secular and Catholic.

Ask them to search through the papers for any pictures or stories that reveal:
  a. Stands on issues or situations taken by Catholics individually, in groups, or by the official representatives.
  b. Stories about individuals who take a prophetic stand against evil of various kinds.

When sufficient data is gathered from the papers, the teams should discuss what they found in relation to the principles discussed in this chapter regarding the Church's prophetic role. After the team discussions, the teams should share their findings with the whole group.

3. *Meditate/Pray:* Invite the group to a period of meditation and prayer. To help create a prayerful atmosphere and initiate meditative reflection on the Church's role as herald, project one striking slide or a series of slides. The visual could show one or more situations crying out for a clear stand and positive action by individual Catholics as well as by the Church as a whole. Very meaningful slides can be made by photographing

situations in your neighborhood or city. Encourage silence during this time.

Then ask one of the group to read Jesus' words as found in Matthew 10:24-33. After the reading, an informal dialogue homily might be a help toward discovering the implication of Jesus' words for the Church and individual Catholics today. End with spontaneous prayer and an appropriate hymn or song.

RESOURCES

Hans Küng shares his views on the Church and its mission in a lecture preserved on two cassettes and entitled *Jesus: Challenge to the Church.* Available from The Thomas More Association, 180 North Wabash Avenue, Chicago, Illinois 60601.

Carl Pfeifer's *Photomeditations* sensitively relate photos of contemporary realities with biblical texts. Available as slides (with printed meditations supplied) from Mark IV Presentations, Attleboro, Mass. 02703) or in book form from Thomas More Association, 180 N. Wabash Avenue, Chicago, Ill. 60601.

READINGS

Avery Dulles, S.J., describes "The Church as Herald," on pages 71-82 of his *Models of the Church* (New York: Doubleday, 1974).

Matthew Fox, O.P., explores the importance of prophecy as a dimension of genuine prayer in Chapter 5 of his stimulating book on prayer, *On Becoming a Musical, Mystical Bear: Spirituality American Style* (New York: Paulist Press, 1976).

The "Dogmatic Constitution on Divine Revelation," in *The Documents of Vatican II,* provides insight into the Church's understanding of God's word in the Church.

Most useful for reading more deeply into the Bible according to its major themes which parallel life experience themes is Xavier Leon-Dufour's *Dictionary of Biblical Theology* (New York: Seabury Press, 1973).

Carl Pfeifer

6

The Church as Servant

I vividly recall the day Pope John died. I was at home in St. Louis. I remember how I listened to the car radio as I drove to visit friends. Frequent bulletins reported the dying Pope's prolonged struggle for life, the slow, painful slipping away of his strength. I remember the unusual sense of compassion, of personal involvement in the voices of the newscasters. It was as if someone very close were dying.

Somehow Pope John XXIII had touched the hearts of people around the world, believers and unbelievers alike. Despite all the pomp and ceremony of his high ecclesiastical position, he communicated a simplicity and a respect for others that attracted people of all faiths, and of no faith. He seemed so human, so much a part of this earth. He conveyed an appreciation for life's joys, an openness to the exciting possibilities of modern developments. His life was marked by compassion for human weakness and appreciation for human achievement. People seemed to feel at home with him because he seemed so much at home with them and the world.

Pope John seemed comfortable in the world while he cherished the Church of which he was the leader. As pope, he taught with authority, but seemed also to listen. He treasured the riches of Catholic tradition, yet conveyed a genuine respect for other traditions. He preached the gospel of Christ yet respected the gospel of all who worked seriously for justice and a better world. While well aware of the evils in the world, Pope John seemed basically optimistic about the modern world and those who people it.

Pope John's personal example and his deliberate actions as Supreme Pontiff initiated a dramatic development in the Church's attitude toward the world in which it lives. His optimistic view, tempered by a realism born of long experience, was expressed in the document with which he convoked the Second Vatican Council: *Distrustful souls see only darkness burdening the face of the earth. We, instead, like to reaffirm all our confidence in our Savior, Who has not left the world which He redeemed.*

The council subsequently elaborated on Pope John's positive appreciation of the world and of human developments. In defining the Church as a "Pilgrim People," sharing life's mysterious journey with everyone else, there is a conscious sense of identification with people in their common search, in their failures and achievements.

Without ever neglecting the evils that exist in every human heart, Vatican Council II stressed that the Church needs to listen with respect for God's word in the world-at-large. Christians, the council teaches, need to be open to insights from other faiths, from modern science, from socio-political movements, even from those who are hostile to the Church and to Jesus Christ. The remarkable *Constitution on the Church in the Modern World* summarizes Pope John's and the council's outlook: "May the faithful, therefore, live in very close union with the men of their time. . . . Let them blend modern science and its theories and the understanding of the most recent discoveries with Christian morality and doctrine. Thus their religious practice and morality can keep pace with their scientific knowledge and with an ever-advancing technology. Thus, too, they will be able to test and interpret all things in a truly Christian spirit" (62).

The reason for the council's respectful attitude toward the modern world is not a matter of improved public relations but of a renewed theology. In opening the council, Pope John had recalled Jesus' own chal-

lenge to learn to read the "signs of the times" (Matthew
16:4) in order to discover God's presence and plan. In
like manner, the council fathers repeatedly affirm that
for the Church to hear God's call and sense the guidance of His Spirit, it needs to turn to world developments and contemporary values as well as to the Bible
and church tradition. The council points out that the
task of bishops and laity alike is to labor to discern
God's presence and activity in the "signs of the times"
(4, 11) and the "voices of our age" (44), and to assess
what they learn there in the light of the gospel.

Such a theological perspective rests on a renewed
awareness of the implications of the doctrines of creation and incarnation. God not only created the world
"in the beginning" but continues that creation through
His creative involvement in human creativity. God's
word not only became flesh in Nazareth centuries ago,
but the Risen Lord remains with us always and everywhere. Everything, everyone can be a medium through
which God speaks and acts in His Son, Jesus.

From Pessimism to Optimism

Such a stance of Church toward the world in which it
finds itself is a dramatic change from the negative
views expressed in official church documents of the
previous century. Pope Pius XI in 1864, felt compelled
to condemn a long list of modern developments in his
famous *Syllabus of Errors.* In 1907, the Church offi-
cially reiterated this pessimism about the world in the
condemnation of Modernism. Pope Pius XII in 1939,
warned Catholics against "handing themselves over to
a capricious ruler, the feeble and grovelling wisdom of
man." His encyclical sums up in its title, *Darkness Over
the Earth,* centuries of official attitudes toward the
world ranging from outright condemnation, to suspi-
cion, to benign neglect.

Pope John and Vatican Council II reversed that trend
by drawing on long forgotten riches of biblical and tra-

ditional teachings as well as new insights of great people like Teilhard de Chardin.

Their renewed appreciation of the religious significance of "secular" reality led to a new insight into the nature of the Church. Existing models of the Church generally suggested a distanced, superior, suspicious stance toward the world. A closer, more respectful, collaborative relation to the modern world provided the initial sketch of a new model of the Church, that of "servant."

The models of the Church considered in previous chapters tend to underplay the world's religious worth. To see the Church, for example, as God's People, chosen and graced, suggests—at least by implication—that holiness and wholeness are to be found within that elect community rather than outside it. The council provided a partial corrective to this basically separatist view of the Church by viewing the People of God as a "Pilgrim People."

The institutional model of the Church with its emphasis on visible criteria of membership further strengthens the sense of separation between Church and world, as well as emphasizes the Church's privileged position. Even the sacrament model of the Church sees the Church as a sign of light and hope to a world marked chiefly by darkness and despair. And the prophetic model views the Church's chief task as preaching God's word to a world tragically in need of redemption.

Church as Servant

Without repudiating in any way the validity of those models of the Church, Vatican Council II suggested a new model of a *servant Church* to reveal a heretofore neglected dimension of the Church's reality. The *servant model* flows from the recognition of the religious validity of the world outside the Church, and the common human search for God's kingdom. Jesus Christ and His Spirit are at work wherever people work for justice, beauty, and true human values. The Church is called to serve all people in discovering and accepting God's kingdom as they work to build a better world. The Second Vatican Council ended with a call to all Christians to join together to "work as brothers in rendering service to the human family" (*Church in World,* 92). The bishops affirm that "Christians cannot yearn for anything more ardently than to serve the men of the modern world even more generously and effectively" (93). The Church has a responsibility to work with everyone of good will to create a more humane world. As such, it sees itself as *servant* rather than triumphalistic master.

But the council did not develop a finished portrait of the *servant Church.* It deftly sketched its outline in broad strokes, suggesting that the Church was to serve the world as Jesus did. He entered the world "to give witness to the truth, to rescue and not to sit in judgment, to serve and not to be served" (*Church in World,* 3). Filling in the details of the portrait needs to be done by considering Jesus' life and teachings in the light of contemporary needs and opportunities.

Jesus as Servant

A careful reading of the gospels reveals that Jesus—without in any way denying His authority or power—quite consciously saw Himself as *servant.* Modern New Testament scholarship has traced the apparent development of Jesus' own self-image as a "suffering servant."

John's Gospel gives us a dramatic portrait of Jesus revealing Himself as servant. It is within the context of Jesus' final meal with His disciples. To their astonishment, He took a bowl of water and a towel and washed their feet—a task normally done by a servant or slave. When He was finished, He urged them to treat one another in the same manner. Just as He, their "Teacher" and "Lord" acted toward them as their servant, so they are to serve one another (John 13:13).

That scene sums up Jesus' whole life. He spent His mature years in the service of others—showing compassion for the poor and the sick, helping the tormented find peace, encouraging the fearful, providing food for the hungry of body and spirit. All His waking hours were at the disposal of anyone in need, to the extent that often He had hardly a moment for Himself. Modern theologians try to capture His spirit by calling Him simply "the man for others."

As best we can get inside the mind of Jesus from gospel accounts, the image of "servant" gradually became a dominant part of His self-image. The gospels reveal Jesus' apparent identification of Himself with the mysterious "suffering servant" described by the prophet Isaiah. The "Servant of the Lord" oracles or poems of Isaiah provide a key to unlocking much of the New Testament (Isaiah 42:1-4; 49:1-7; 50:4-11; 52:13-53:12).

In chiding His quarreling disciples about their petty ambition, Jesus reveals His own self-ideal in words that echo Isaiah's description of the servant who takes upon himself the sins of the people. "Anyone among you," Jesus tells His friends, "who aspires to greatness must serve the rest. . . . The Son of Man has not come to be served, but to serve—to give His life in ransom for the many" (Mark 10:44-45).

Directly quoting Isaiah, Matthew's Gospel characterizes Jesus' compassion toward the sick in terms of service: "Here is my servant whom I have chosen" (Matthew 12:18-21; Isaiah 42:1). The same text is cited by Matthew, Mark, and Luke in their accounts of Jesus' baptism, but the word "servant" is there changed to "son" (Matthew 3:17; Mark 1:11; Luke 3:22).

In Luke's Gospel (4:16-22) Jesus is described as reading a similar passage from Isaiah (61:1) aloud in the Nazareth synagogue. It is about bringing sight to

the blind, freedom to captives, and good news to the
poor—the same themes as the earlier servant-poems
mentioned above. He concluded the reading by an-
nouncing that Isaiah's words are fulfilled in Him.
Many more texts could be cited to show how central
the image of "servant" is to the New Testament understanding of Jesus. It seems that the image originated
with Jesus Himself Who interpreted His life and mission in terms of Isaiah's vision of a "suffering servant
of the Lord."

A Servant Church

Curiously the image of *servant* was not applied explicitly to the Church as a whole—as a model for understanding the Church—until the Second Vatican
Council. Down through the centuries, individual Christians and communities of Christians have dedicated
their lives to the service of others, in imitation of Jesus.
The term "servant" became a formal phrase associ-
ated with the pope: "Servant of the servants of all." But
in relation to the world-at-large, the Church as such
was not seen clearly as "servant." In fact, in the Middle
Ages, the pope crowned the emperor whose empire
was more at the service of the Church than *vice versa*.
Even in the New Testament, there is no explicit naming
of the Church as a "servant church" in its dealings with
the world.

Yet the Church of Jesus Christ is the extension in
time and space of Jesus and His mission. It is appropriate that the Church today take on the self-image of its
master Who saw Himself as servant.

The implications of this original contribution of the
Second Vatican Council are vast for the Church and
for individual Christians. Most obvious is a change of
heart, a new attitude toward all men and women who
strive to create a more wholesome world, an attitude of
respect, of growing understanding and collaboration.
The servant model suggests a Church much more

humble and open to modern developments in so many aspects of life. It points toward serious changes in some of the Church's external trappings and operational styles.

Some of these changes have become a reality since the council. There have been signs of more genuine and closer collaboration with men and women of good will whatever their religious beliefs. The official Church has shown greater openness toward the discoveries of the social and physical sciences. There appears a less triumphalistic stance toward the rest of the world, with indications of genuine respect for the traditions of others.

But the servant model presents even greater spiritual and organizational challenges in the future. The Church as a whole, and each Christian individually, falls far short of the ideal of generous service Jesus Himself presents us. Perhaps the image of Pope John provides some of the best clues as to how the Church, without relinquishing its responsibility as teacher, herald, or sacrament, can more effectively, more humanly be at the service of the rest of humankind.

SUGGESTED ACTIVITIES

Primary Level

1. *Share examples:* Share with the children the example of someone outstanding in their attitude of Christian service. Pope John XXIII or Mother Teresa are obvious examples. Other less famous Christians, even persons the children know, may be more meaningful. Use any pictures or other media that you can find to make the story more interesting.

Take time to get the children's reactions to the people's lives and messages.

2. *Draw:* Tell the children one or more stories of how Jesus went about helping others, serving their needs.

Then ask them to draw or paint pictures that show Jesus as *servant* or *helper.*

When they finish, display their pictures and invite them to look at and talk about them. Help them grow in appreciation of how selfless and compassionate Jesus is.

3. *Find Photos:* Give the children a large selection of photos that you have found in magazines and newspapers (or have the children find the pictures themselves). Ask them to look through the photos and select the one that reminds them most of Jesus. Invite each to show his or her selected photo and tell why it reminds him or her of Jesus.

Intermediate Level

1. *Trace history of Christian service:* Invite the students to look into the history of the Church's works of service. Many of what now are public, social works supported by the government originated as practical expressions of Christian service. Have them look into

the history of hospitals, hotels for travellers, homes for orphans and the poor, soup kitchens, etc.

Have them translate their findings into one or more attractive, compelling visual presentations of Christian service.

2. *Take Field Trip:* Find a local example of Christian service to those in need. Take the youngsters on a tour of the place, with ample opportunity to meet and talk with those engaged in the ministry of service.

After the field trip, have the youngsters draw up personal or group reports on their experience. Help them relate what they observed with the example and message of Jesus as *servant.*

3. *Study Bible:* Share with the youngsters the references found in the chapter that refer to Jesus' own use of the *servant* model. Have them look up and discuss these passages—individually or in small teams.

Challenge them then to come up with a composite verbal portrait of *Jesus the Servant.* Help them relate Jesus' example and message to the Church today and to their own lives.

Secondary Level

1. *Discuss:* Divide your group into small teams of four to six individuals. After discussing the contents of this chapter, allow at least 30 minutes for discussion of the key ideas. The teams may then report to the whole group their own insights and feelings generated by their discussion. They might also add their own questions that remain unanswered. The whole group could then discuss further any issues that seem to be of more common concern.

It might be helpful after the discussion to go back and review the significant ideas in the chapter.

2. *Meditate/Pray:* Encourage a quiet atmosphere for

prayer and meditation. Soft music might provide a helpful background and atmosphere. A projected slide might provide a visual focus, for example, one of Jesus washing His disciples' feet, or responding to the sick and needy, or of people serving the needs of people today. Then read aloud slowly either John 13:1-17, or Isaiah 52:13-53:12, or both. Allow time for silent reflection and prayer. Encourage spontaneous prayer if the group is comfortable with that. Perhaps create a litany of petitions that the Church in various ways becomes more and more like *Jesus the servant.* Close with an appropriate hymn.

3. *Evaluate Church as Servant:* Divide the group into smaller working teams. Give them the task of discovering and evaluating the Church they know against the model of Servant Church. Challenge them to be as objective as possible, documenting where possible, and grounding their evaluation in relation to the biblical or Vatican II images of servant.

When they have finished, and have all shared their evaluations, urge them to suggest concrete, practical ways the Church—and they as individuals, may develop more fully according to the servant model.

Adult Level

1. *Read Signs of the Times:* Pope John popularized the term "signs of the times," used by Jesus in the gospels (Matthew 16:4). Vatican Council II took up the usage and since the council it has been used frequently to describe indications of God's presence and guidance in the happenings or trends or developments in the contemporary world. (See *Church in World,* 4, 11, and "voices of our age" in 44.)

After the group has listened to your presentation, invite them—individually or in small teams—to list modern developments they feel might be "signs of the times" in the positive sense that Pope John and the council used.

To make their search more realistic you might provide them with assorted newspapers and magazines as resources. To make their lists more attractive and meaningful they could create collages or posters entitled "Signs of the Times." Instead of newspapers and magazines, collections of slides might be the resource for creating a slide-sound collage with the same title.

In the process of their work they might look up the texts cited above from the gospel and the council documents. Parts of these texts could be incorporated in their creative lists.

2. *Study Texts:* Assign individuals to look at some of the actual biblical and Vatican Council texts relative to the *servant model* of the Church. The following are some of the more important:

Bible: The basic sources are the mysterious "Servant Songs" found in Isaiah: 42:1-4; 49:1-7; 50:4-11; 52:13-53:12. Similar to the original servant-poems is Isaiah 61:1-3.

New Testament references to the Servant theme of Isaiah are many. Some of the more important ones are these: John 13:13; Mark 10:44-45; Luke 4:16-22; Matthew 12:18-21. The model sermons of Peter in the Acts of the Apostles refer to Jesus as servant: 3:13, 26; 4:27, 30. The descriptions of Jesus' Baptism draw upon the servant-poems of Isaiah, but use the word son as an alternative to servant: Matthew 3:17; Mark 1:11; Luke 3:22. So, too, in describing the Transfiguration: Matthew 17:5; Mark 9:7; Luke 9:35.

Documents of Vatican II: Constitution on the Church in the Modern World: 3, 92, 93.

Note: For further resources on the Servant theme in the scriptures see "Servant of God" in John L. McKenzie's *Dictionary of the Bible,* or in Xavier Leon-Dufour's *Dictionary of Biblical Theology.*

3. *Finish the Portrait:* The council simply sketched the

lines of a portrait of the *Church as Servant.* Jesus' life helps fill in the major details. Your group could try to flesh out the *servant model* more fully by taking a hard look at the Church as they know it—on the parish, diocesan, national or universal levels.

Have them work in small groups to discover actual indications that the Church is increasingly reflecting the image of *servant* in relation to the world-at-large. Their search may also reveal traces of attitudes or positions that seem at odds with the servant model. Both positive and negative should be honestly noted and discussed.

They might pull together their impressions by creating some kind of visual expression of the Church as servant—a collage or poster, for example.

RESOURCES

Mother Teresa of Calcutta is a moving model of service to those in need. *These Are My People* beautifully conveys her example and message in a seven-minute, 51-frame color filmstrip (Franciscan Communications Center, 1229 S. Santee Street, Los Angeles, Ca. 90015).

A cassette study course on Church renewal, *New Life for the Church,* (13 programs on seven cassettes) with illustrated study guide by Dr. Edward W. Bauman is available (Bauman Media Associates, 3436 Lee Highway, Arlington, Va. 22207).

READINGS

Avery Dulles, S.J., describes "The Church as Servant" on pages 83-96 of his classic book, *Models of the Church* (Doubleday, Garden City, N.Y. 11531).

Constitution on the Church in the Modern World, in the *Documents of Vatican II,* especially numbers 1-4, 11, 40-45, 53-62, 92-93.

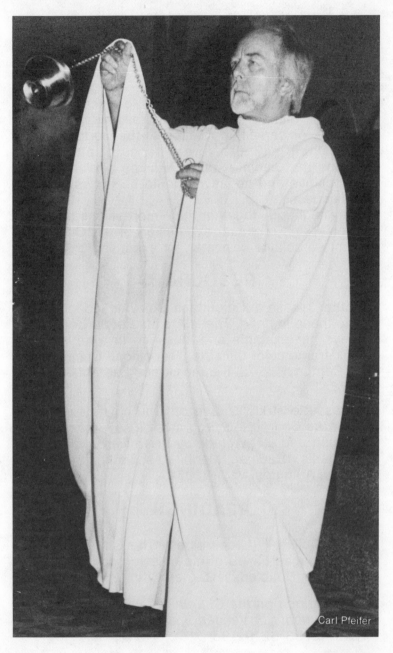

Carl Pfeifer

7

The Church as Worshipper

I once asked a group of 5th graders what their religion was. They answered without hesitation, "Catholic." "How do you know you are Catholics?" I pressed them. "We go to St. Agnes church," was their reply.

We talked about their friends and playmates. Were they all Catholic? No. It seemed some were Baptists, others Methodists, but most were Catholics. How did they know a Baptist? Well, obviously, Baptists were their friends who went to the nearby Baptist Church. Their Methodist friends went to the Methodist Church down the street. They reassured me they were Catholics—because they went to St. Agnes church.

I thought about that conversation for a long time. In many ways it was very superficial. It revealed how youngsters think very concretely and experientially. But it didn't seem too deep theologically. Catholics went to Catholic Churches, Baptists to Baptist Churches, and Methodists to Methodist Churches. True, observable, but what does it tell you about being a Catholic, Baptist or Methodist?

After some reflection, it become clear that the youngsters, perhaps superficially and unwittingly, were putting their finger on precisely what it is that reveals the identity of Christians in general and Catholics, Baptists or Methodists in particular. In fact, they were pointing to what ultimately identifies every believer and every religion. Worship!

It has been said that a human being is most himself or herself when kneeling before God. It is equally true that the Church is most truly itself—Church—when at worship. Christians are most evidently united with—yet distinguished from—Buddhists or Hindus in their worship. Christians of all churches are most closely united, while remaining separate, in their worship of God in Jesus name. Church is most evidently Church when it is at worship.

The youngsters obviously could not understand or explain this, but their perception was sure. They knew they were Catholics because they—and their families—went to St. Agnes church. Why did they go there? To worship God. In that community worship lay the clue to their identity. They sensed this before being able to understand it.

Church Born in Worship

Before all else, the Church of Jesus Christ is a worshipping community. It has many other tasks—being a prophet or light to the world, serving the individual and social needs of people, providing guidance and opportunities for holiness to its own members—but its most basic task as Church is to pray, to worship God, the Father of Jesus Christ, in Jesus name. Church is primarily a community at worship.

In worship it was born. The Spirit of Christ came to the disciples in the place where, after Jesus' ascension, "together they devoted themselves to constant prayer" (Acts 1:14). Filled with the Spirit that Pentecost morning, they immediately began to pray in tongues. So Luke portrays the birth of the Church.

John describes the Church's birth even more profoundly. He sees the Church born out of Jesus' final, total, act of worship on the cross. Symbolically, John describes Jesus' death as a complete giving over of Himself to the Father: "Then He bowed His head, and delivered over His Spirit" (John 19:30). Through a deliberate play on words, Jesus' worshipful handing over to God of His Spirit, is also described as a sending of the Spirit. The giving up is at the same time a pouring out—of the Holy Spirit.

The Spirit is sent forth to draw all men and women into Jesus' act of total worship. The Church is born at that moment. John describes the birth of the Church, symbolically, in terms of the blood and water flowing from the pierced side of the Crucified. (John 19:34). This ancient patristic interpretation of the birth of the Church from the open wound in the side of the Crucified is repeated in Vatican Council II's description of the mystery of the Church (Church, 3). The Council highlights the Church's union with Jesus' ultimate act of worship. From its birth, the Church is essentially called to worship.

Church at Worship

And from its earliest days, the communities of Christians gathered to worship God in Jesus' name. The Acts of the Apostles records how from the beginning, "They devoted themselves to the apostles' instruction and the communal life, to the breaking of bread and the prayers" (Acts 2:42). They went daily to the Temple to pray, and in their homes they celebrated the "breaking of bread," the Lord's Supper, the Eucharist. Worship was at the heart of their lives as individuals and as communities.

This image of Christians as worshippers is found also in the earliest Roman document describing the Christian communities. Pliny, the chief Roman official in Bithynia, wrote to the Emperor Trajan around the year 100 A.D. He claims to have investigated the Christian way of life to discover if it was contrary to Roman laws. His description of the Christians centers on their worship. "They met regularly in the early morning on a fixed day to chant hymns in honor of Christ, as if to a god. They took oaths to remain faithful to their wives and husbands, and not to steal or cheat. After the ceremony they shared food together at a common meal."

From those early days, the Church has continually been at worship. Catacombs, churches, cathedrals, chapels dot the globe as evidence of the worshipping presence of the Church in ages past as well as today. We used to boast that there was a Mass being offered somewhere in the world every moment of the day. The hours of day and night have been and continue to be sanctified as prayerful men and women pray the Divine Office. Prayer is like the Church's life-sustaining, life-sharing breath.

Church for Worship

The Second Vatican Council placed considerable emphasis on the fact that the Church's worship is ultimately the reason for its existence. The Church is most itself when praying. In its first official document, the Council states that the "liturgy is ... the outstanding means by which the faithful can express in their lives, and manifest to others the mystery of Christ and the real nature of the Church" (*Constitution on the Sacred Liturgy, 2*).

Later in the same document, a fuller description is given. The Council Fathers teach "that the Church reveals herself most clearly when a full complement of God's holy people, united in prayer and in a common liturgical service (especially the Eucharist), exercise a thorough and active participation at the very altar where the bishop presides in the company of his priests and other assistants" (41). The Church at worship—with all involved according to their respective roles—is what the Church is really most profoundly about. It is gathered *for* worship. From worship all else is to be enlivened. The Church is—using a biblical image—Christ's "dearly beloved Bride who calls to her Lord, and through Him offers worship to the Eternal Father" (7).

The Council later went on to describe the Church's many other roles in its relationship with all of mankind. As *Prophet,* the Church is to stand up and speak out against evil of all kinds. As *Servant,* the Church is to minister to the needs of a broken world and build upon the creative forces at work to fashion a better world. As *Institution,* the Church is to preserve basic truths and vital values, not just for its members but for the whole of humankind. As *Pilgrim,* the Church is to learn from and walk with all those searching out a way to life's deepest meaning and lasting happiness.

But that and all else in the Church is meant to draw its life from and breathe back ever new life into the Church as *Worshipper.*

Renewal in Worship

Because worship is the life-breath of the Church, so much attention since Vatican Council II has been given to liturgical renewal. The rites for all the sacraments have been revised in an effort to encourage and enrich community worship. In some respects, this effort has been sporadic and poorly planned. In places liturgical renewal has been merely superficial. But where careful planning and sensitive implementation occur, communities have experienced in their lives what the Council described in its documents.

Parishes in every part of our country have come alive through renewal of parish worship. Parishioners have come to re-discover through meaningful worship together what it means to be a Christian, a Catholic. In such parishes, worship is central to an overall renewal that builds a sense of community within the parish and a sense of commitment to the world at large. Through more active, responsible involvement in the liturgy, men and women have discovered a new sense of identity. They have come to know they are Catholics and what it means to be a Catholic "by going to St. Agnes church."

Those youngsters sensed that it is in their local community at worship that they and their parents discover who they are as Catholics. For it is there in a worshipping community that the Church most fully takes shape and reveals itself.

Mary, Model of Church

Perhaps that is a major reason that the Church sees Mary as its ideal model (*Constitution on the Church,* 53, 63). Mary's whole life, as revealed in the gospels, is characterized by worship, by an openness, a responsiveness to God's word in her life. Her life is a lived *Magnificat,* a lived liturgy of praise and thanks. And at the end she stands at the foot of the cross, sharing her Son's final act of loving worship.

She is the model of the Church, gathered in openness to God's word, praising and thanking Him for His goodness and graciousness, pleading before Him for all who are in need. Mary, at the side of the Crucified, images the Church at its deepest level where it unites itself with the sacrificial worship of its unique High Priest, Jesus Christ.

Christians have long created artistic images of Mary in varying stances of prayer. Traditionally, the Church has known itself as Worshipper. The New Testament, the early Church Fathers, and the Second Vatican Council therefore see Mary as the ideal, the model, of the Church. For the Church, before all else, exists to worship, to pray.

"Know that the Lord is God;
he made us, his we are;
his people, the flock he tends.

Enter his gates with thanksgiving,
his courts with praise;

Give thanks to him; bless his name,
for he is good:
the Lord, whose kindness endures forever,
and his faithfulness, to all generations. (Psalm 100)

SUGGESTED ACTIVITIES

Primary Level

1. *Learn Traditional Prayers:* Review with, or teach, the children some of the Church's "traditional" prayers—prayers that provide important touchstones of the Church's worship—e.g., Sign of the Cross, Our Father, Hail Mary, Glory Be. Others like the Apostles' Creed, the Jesus Prayer, short prayers from the Mass may also be learned—but only according to the capacities of the children. Do not overburden them with prayer formulae, but it is valuable to them to be familiar with the prayers most characteristic of our public worship.

Once they have learned a prayer by heart, be sure to lead them in praying it reverently from time to time—not just as a "drill" or "review" but as actual prayer at appropriate moments.

2. *Learn Other Prayers:* Guide the children to more spontaneous and varied expressions of prayer. Help them become aware that God is always with us and that we may always recognize and respond to His presence if we wish. Help them learn short prayers from the Psalms, e.g., "I will give thanks to you, O Lord, with all my heart" (Psalm 9:2), "O Lord, my God, you are great indeed" (Psalm 104:1), "O Lord, be my helper." (Psalm 30:11), "Have mercy on me, O God, in your goodness" (Psalm 51:3), "O Lord, my God, in you I trust" (Psalm 25:1-2), "I love you, O Lord, my strength" (Psalm 18:2), etc.

With these as models, encourage the children to express similar prayers in their own words. Jot these down for them and for future use with them.

3. *Pray with Media:* Help the children broaden and deepen their experience of prayer by having them use media. For example, invite them to pray non-verbally,

"O God, our Father, you are wonderful." They might pray this prayer of praise with bodily movements, gesture or dance. They might pray it with drawing or painting, or by collecting pictures that suggest their reasons for praising God. Be creative with them and help them through their creative expression come to *feel* praise and express it.

Intermediate Level

1. *Visit Church:* Visit the parish church with the youngsters. Ask them to go all around the church with paper and pencil, or drawing paper and crayons, or cameras, in search of anything that suggests that this is a "house of prayer" designed for the community to worship in. Have them note down or draw everything that seems an aid to worship.

Afterwards, let them share what they noted and talk about the fact that Catholics and other Christians come together frequently to worship. Help them recognize that prayer is at the heart of being Christian.

2. *Create Visual Presentations:* Share with the youngsters the ideas in the chapter. Then challenge them to present creatively an interpretation of the Church as worshipping community. They might make a collage, using photos from various religious and other magazines, or a bulletin board display, a slide-sound show, or a large mural, or some other form of audio, visual or audio-visual presentation.

3. *Introduce Liturgical Times:* Share with the youngsters the major divisions of the liturgical year. Make use of a liturgical calendar. Or make a large chart on which you can point out the major seasons and the major feasts in each season. Explain the importance of Sunday. Then share with them some knowledge of the Divine Office, prayed day and night, to sanctify the entire day.

A priest or monk might be willing to come as a guest speaker. In this way, help them recognize how comprehensive is the reality of Church as worshipping community.

Secondary Level

1. *Respond to Photos:* Give the group a selection of photographs or slides of persons praying—Christians and believers of other religions. Let small teams select the photo that to them best suggests the meaning of worship or prayer.

Allow each team to share its findings and reasons with the whole group. Then guide them more deeply into the value and meaning of prayer, as they see it, and as you see it. Draw upon experience. Help them broaden their grasp of the Church as a praying community, using some of the data presented in the chapter, and in the biblical or Vatican II texts it cites.

Invite them individually to write prayers, which then may be prayed in a brief prayer experience. Include a song or hymn, like Joe Wise's "Lord Teach us to Pray," *A New Day* (World Library of Sacred Music, 2145 Central Pkwy, Cincinnati, Ohio 45214).

2. *Celebrate Special Liturgy:* After discussing the ideas in the chapter, invite the group to prepare and celebrate a special liturgy on the theme of *Church as Worshipper* or worshipping community. Encourage them to select scripture (and perhaps non-biblical) readings, appropriate songs, suitable gestures, create banners or a slide presentation, etc. Invite a priest who is at home with and understands youth to celebrate the liturgy with them.

3. *Study Prayer Forms:* Encourage the group to investigate the many forms of worship that are part of the rich spiritual tradition of the Church. In a time of heightened interest in meditation and prayer among

the young, and a curiosity about Oriental prayer forms, it would be marvellous for a group to do an extended research and creative project on Christian prayer.

Adult Level

1. *Discussion:* Encourage honesty and sharing of personal experience as the following questions are discussed: *To what extent do you agree that the Church is most itself when at worship? How have you experienced this in your own life? Why is the Church primarily a worshipping community? What is the relationship between worship and the other activities of the Church? What difference does it make if you have good liturgy or not in your parish? How does Mary strike you as a model of the Church?*

Only in an atmosphere of trust and understanding will adults be open about their real ideas and feelings about their own and the Church's worship.

End the discussion with a brief prayer experience that draws upon the major themes of their discussion.

2. *Invite Guest Lecturer:* Invite in someone who has wide knowledge and experience of prayer in the Church—its importance, its various forms, its private and liturgical expressions, its relation to forms of meditation and prayer which have recently captured the interest of so many.

Encourage the group to question the speaker honestly and probingly. Be sure there is adequate time for discussion.

3. *Create Worship Experience:* Few adults have much experience in creating group prayer experiences. Invite them to design a prayer service they feel would be very meaningful and would express the reality of the Church as a worshipping community. They might design their own liturgical celebration, inviting a priest to celebrate the Eucharist with them, or they might prefer a "para-liturgical" service without a priest.

RESOURCES

Helpful periodic resources on understanding theory and practice of worship in the Church are *Today's Parish* (Twenty-Third Publications, Box 180, West Mystic, CT 06388), *Liturgy* (Liturgical Conference, 1221 Massachusetts Ave., N. W., Washington, D.C. 20005), *Modern Liturgy* (Resource Publications, PO Box 444, Saratoga, CA 95070), *Worship* (St. John Abbey, Collegeville, Minn. 56321), *Pastoral Music* (1029 Vermont Ave., N.W., Washington, D.C.), *National Bulletin on Liturgy,* (National Liturgical Office, 90 Parent Ave., Ottawa, Ont KIN7VL).

The Mass is a four-part filmstrip explaining the Eucharist as we celebrate today. Designed for teens and adults. (23rd Publications, West Mystic, Ct. 06388).

READINGS

Dry Bones: Living Worship Guides to Good Liturgy by Robert W. Hovda provides sound pastoral reflection and guidelines for Church worship (Liturgical Conference, 1221 Massachusetts Ave., N.W., Washington, D.C. 20005). Other helpful books from the same source are Robert W. Hovda's *Strong, Loving and Wise: Presiding in Liturgy,* and two books edited by Virgina Sloyan, *Signs, Songs and Stories: Another Look at Children's Liturgies,* and *Liturgy Committee Handbook: A Nine-Week Study Guide.*

George Devine evaluates worship in the Church in *Liturgical Renewal: An Agonizing Reappraisal* (New York: Alba House, 1973, 2187 Victory Blvd., Staten Island, N.Y. 10314).

Anthony Padavano's *A Case for Worship* and Carl J. Pfeifer and Janaan Manternach's *A Case for Faith,* both from the Silver Burdett Religious Education Program (Morristown, New Jersey: Silver Burdett Company, 1978) provide balanced ideas and practical helps in exploring the Church as worshipper.

Carl Pfeifer

8

The Church as Multimedia

About five years ago I bought my first camera. It was a simple Instamatic. I was going on a trip and wanted some snapshots as souvenirs of people and places. I had no idea what an influence on my life that purchase was to make.

My whole education had been taken up with words—reading, writing, literature, languages, philosophy, theology. I had spent most of my education listening to words, reading words, writing words. I was at home with books, comfortable—if bored at times—with lectures. I had become saturated with verbal communication.

As a result, my own efforts at communication centered on the written and spoken word. I was becoming somewhat skilled at the same verbal communication in which I was educated. I experienced and respected the power of words.

Then I bought a camera. I began looking at life through its viewfinder, rather than through the medium of words alone. It was an exciting experience. I began noticing many things that I had previously passed by without noticing. I found that even a souvenir snapshot could bring back memories, touch the imagination, and stir feelings in a way that words were unable to do.

I was also discovering how helpful photos could be in my religious education work with adults and children. Photos provided a unique window into reality, one through which several could look at once and see different depths and riches. Photos invited involvement and stimulated dialogue. They also were marvelous for meditation and prayer.

With the discovery of photography I was also becoming much more sensitive to the power of art—painting, architecture, sculpture, dance, music, film—to communicate delightfully in depth. I began to use these media in my efforts at communication in workshops, lectures, teaching and praying. I found that people responded more fully, more meaningfully to a sensitive blend of verbal and non-verbal communication.

My personal experience obviously was but a minute part of what people everywhere seemed to be experiencing. We have all been affected by a massive media development closely related to the electronic breakthroughs that made television and computers an everyday reality. Marshall McLuhan prophetically—if somewhat prematurely—predicted the demise of the linear, print culture and the rise of a whole new electronic culture, with the electronic communications media creating a new language, which in turn was creating a new world, which was already becoming a global village. He coined the famous phrase to describe the revolutionary nature of the media explosion: "The medium *is* the message." New media are not merely new ways of communicating the same old message; they are a part of the message itself.

The Church could not remain unaffected by so dramatic and widespread a cultural development. Vatican Council II published a decree on the *Instruments of Social Communication.* Unfortunately, it was probably the council's least impressive document. Later, the Vatican issued a more substantial instruction on communications. An international meeting on the subject of media and communications was held in the United States. The American hierarchy has had annual institutes for bishops on communications. The Church was attempting to become more aware of the impact and opportunities of the new media revolution.

But what about the Church itself? Do the new communications media merely provide new means of communicating the message of Christ? Or does the contemporary concern with communications suggest something about the very nature of the Church itself? If the world of human experience is affected by the electronic age, is the Church also? If the medium is the message, what kind of challenge does the message of Jesus pose to the Church as its privileged medium?

At the 1971 Bishops' Communications Institute in New Orleans, the American theologian, Avery Dulles, S.J., delivered a significant paper entitled, "The Church as Multimedia." He insightfully suggested that the media revolution of our time provides insights into the very nature of the Church as medium of Christ's life and message. His thought substantially guides what follows.

Medium Is Message

All of the models of the Church we have so far considered—*pilgrim people, institution, sacrament, herald, servant, worshipper*—suggest that the Church is a community or communion of people whose purpose is to create and deepen unity among themselves, others and God. Father Dulles concludes that "if communications is seen as the procedure by which communion is achieved and maintained, we may also say that the Church is communications." To define the Church *as communications* touches on the reality of the Church and its role in uniting people with God in Christ and with one another in Christ.

The idea of Church *as communications* or *as multimedia* rests on the fact that the Church is the extension of Jesus Christ in time and space. He is the Word, the self-communication of God's gracious love and divine life, the communicator of the Father. Jesus Christ is the perfect realization of the medium *being* the message. The Church as Incarnate Word extended through the world of space and time shares in this quality of communicator of the Father's life and love. It is essentially medium, or better, media—multimedia. As extension of the Word, the Church not only uses media of communications but is itself a unique communications medium. Such a model is closely related to that of the Church as sign or sacrament.

Just as Jesus communicated the Father's message and life through a variety of media—notably His life, death, and resurrection—so the Church exercises her nature as communicator in a multi-media fashion. The media are conditioned greatly by the cultures in which they exist. The Church's structure, style and even its manner of being are to a greater or lesser extent affected by the communications patterns of the culture in which it exists.

We know Jesus as God's Word, but we err if we identify His revelatory role with His verbal teaching alone. Undoubtedly, Jesus was a master of words. We still marvel at the profundity and beauty of His teachings. But we also gain insight into the Father's life and love by watching Jesus as He moved about the cities and hamlets of Palestine.

For example, we see the Father's mercy in Jesus' forgiveness of sinners as well as in His words about his Father's mercy. Adultress, prostitute, corrupt tax collector, convicted criminal, betrayer, unfaithful friends— all experienced the tenderness of Jesus' forgiveness. Sometimes, it is through a word, at other times through a glance, a kiss, a touch, an embrace. As Word, Jesus is multi-media, with the media of His age.

Likewise the Church. Continuing the mission of Jesus, being intimately united and identified with the Word Incarnate, the Church *is* essentially communicator and essentially multi-media. It communicates, as did Jesus, through what it is, what it does, how it appears, as well as through what it says. *The narrow focus in recent Church history on doctrinal teaching as the chief mode of communicating Christ's message to the world is an impoverishment of the rich modes of communication that the Church has traditionally used.*

St. Paul rightly taught that faith comes through hearing (Romans 10:17), but three centuries later an experienced catechist, bishop and Father of the Church, St. Cyril of Jerusalem, told his people that "faith by seeing is stronger than faith by hearing." The Word is not expressed exclusively through words, although words, particularly the inspired words of the scriptures always retain a unique place in the Church's communication efforts.

Over the centuries, the Church's means of communications paralleled those of the cultures in which it existed. With extreme superficiality we may summarize three major communications modes that developed in the Western World. There was a shift from the spoken word to the written word—preserved in manuscripts—to the printed word of books. Each of the cultural eras not only strongly affected the Church's manner of sharing its message, but helped shape the Church itself as the primary medium. Obviously in all eras the Church shared its insights in other ways than through words, for example in art, music, theater, life-style, community life, social action, architecture, worship, dramatic actions.

But each of these major periods of verbal communication—spoken, written, printed—although supplemented by other audio, visual, tactile and spacial media, strongly affected the shape of the Church itself as the major medium of Christ's message. Avery Dulles traces three broad approaches to the Church's self-understanding that are closely related to the cultural changes in the communications media.

He speaks of a *hierarchical-scholastic* ecclesiology, in which the Church is seen primarily as a hierarchic institution, speaking with authority in the language of abstract, scholastic philosophy. Precision of the theological definition supported hierarchic authority within a Church viewed chiefly as a divinely grounded institution. Manuscript and print cultures fed such a church style and structure. Written and printed words dominated ecclesiastical communications.

The culture of the spoken word—even when that spoken word may find a written or printed counterpart—gave rise to an ecclesiology Dulles calls *biblical-kerygmatic.* The emphasis is on the spoken witness of individuals and communities, a witness to God's involvement in their own lives as well as in the lives of those recorded in the Bible. Conviction, enthusiasm, experience are valued more than scholastic precision. Authority comes not so much from office as from experience of the Spirit. The spoken word is the most apt medium for a personally assimilated message. Community is more significant for witness than is institution.

Finally, Dulles speaks of an ecclesiology—sketched rather than developed in the Second Vatican Council—that he calls *secular dialogic.* It is influenced by the rise of the electronic communications media. Such media of mass social communications affect the Church's self-image and its style and structure. The immediacy and impact of the new visual media demand a new form of authority and witness. They invite participation and encourage dialogue. Though open to manipulation, they call for honesty, respect and humility. Satellite communication unites the world instantly with immediate impact and with power—all within the familiarity of one's home. The Word, more so now than in previous eras of more linear, verbal culture, must take flesh also in images, colors, sounds. More, too, perhaps than in the past, that Word is to be found in the broad "secular" world of human experience as well as within the experience of the Church community.

If that is true, the implications for the Church are vast. Secular-dialogic communication best flows from an inner mindset of broad respect, openness and honesty, and a sincere desire for dialogue, the outcome of which is not unilaterally predetermined. Such attitudes demand a change of heart, a new style of leadership. The Church in an electronic age—without in any way losing the riches of its hierarchical-scho-lastic and biblical-kerygmatic life-styles and commu-nications modes—needs to *be* and *communicate* in a new, humbler, more respectful manner. New styles of being and communicating are needed that are both in greater harmony with the Church's nature as a Pilgrim People and with the marvelous new communications media.

Few insights into the Church's present situation seem so pastorally challenging—personally and cor-porately—than the awareness of the *Church as com-munications or multi-media.* The history of the Church reveals how new communications methods deeply affected the Church's self-understanding, life-style and structure. The new discoveries of mass media social communications that are ushering in an elec-tronic era are as rich in opportunities for the Church and for its message as were the discoveries of writing and printing.

But the adaptation involved in the shift from one pre-dominant cultural form of communications—spoken word, written word, printed word, electronic media—to another is not superficial. It implies not only the learn-ing of new technical skills, but touches at the very heart of Catholics' self-image and attitudes to the world about them. Searching for God's footsteps in the secular world was not part of our upbringing. Nor was respectful and expectant dialogue with those of other faiths or of no faith—or of other ranks or ideologies within the Church itself.

To consider Church as multi-media is a challenge to renewal. I experienced the seeds of this when I began looking through the lens of a camera and discovering in slides and photographs the previously unseen riches of people and things around me. I also dis-covered the photo's potential for dialogue. A photo-graph may make a statement, but it invites a response and dialogue. It brings everyone to a similar level of sharing.

Perhaps the camera and photograph may symbolize the secular-dialogic mode of the Church's being just as preacher and book symbolize its biblical-kerygmatic and hierarchical-scholastic modes. We need them all.

SUGGESTED ACTIVITIES

Primary Level

1. *Share a Child's Book:* Share with the children Leo Lionni's *Frederick* (Pantheon Books, 201 E. 50 St., New York, N.Y. 10022). It is usually available in most book stores in the children's section. A 6-minute color film version also by Leo Lionni is available from Connecticut Films, Inc., 6 Cobble Hill Rd., Westport, CT 06880.

Read the book or show the film to your children. Then invite their reactions, guiding them to talk about what the story says to them about Frederick, about themselves, about life. Help them note the effect on the mice of Frederick's use of colors as well as words. Guide them to see how people communicate with one another about what is important to them in words, visual images, gestures, etc.

Ask them if the Church does this, too. Help them see that the Church approaches us all through words, pictures, art, music, gesture, etc.

2. *Do Something Creative:* Help the children share something beautiful in a creative, multi-media way. If they have enjoyed the story of *Frederick,* suggest that they imitate Frederick. The idea is for them to notice something beautiful in themselves, in others, in the world around them, and attempt to share it with others—by creating a beautiful environment, by drawing a picture, writing a short poem or paragraph, finding and pasting up pictures, etc.

When they finish, let them share what they have done, and talk about their experience. Then share with them how Jesus used stories and poetic words, pointed out beautiful things around Him, moved and acted in such a way that people sensed how loving and compassionate He was. Help them see, too, how the Church uses words, art, music, gesture, movement, dance, photos, etc., to tell us about Jesus and our lives.

Intermediate Level

1. *Examine Sacred Art:* Share with the youngsters as wide a selection of sacred art as you can gather—from various periods of history and from various countries and cultures. Museums and libraries have sometimes large collections of such art in reproduction as slides and/or prints, either free or for very reasonable fees. Excellent art books may be borrowed from libraries or purchased at good bookstores, usually at very large reductions after they have been out a year or two.

Make these available to the youngsters for their study. If possible, prepare an exhibit of one Gospel story or event, e.g., Last Supper, and present 10 or 12 varying depictions of it from around the world and over the centuries.

From their observations, guide them to recognize how important art is in conveying the message of Jesus and the meaning of the Church. Help them discover what the various artists seem to believe and want to say about Jesus and the Church. Make use of the ideas in the chapter as you guide their conversation.

2. *Meditate/Pray:* An appropriate form of prayer suitable to the theme of the *Church as communications or multi-media* would be a period of contemplative appreciation of the immediate world. Create a climate of relaxed quiet. Allow movement that facilitates seeing, hearing, touching, smelling. Appealing instrumental music such as Neil Diamond's *Jonathan Livingston Seagull* would be very appropriate.

After sufficient time for quiet contemplation, read or sing Psalm 104, a hymn of praise to the creator, or Psalms 147 or 148.

An appropriate prayerful response would be to paint or draw an expression of praise to God in whatever art form the group prefers.

Secondary Level

1. *Take pictures:* Invite the group to go out and photograph anything they see which says to them what the Church is, ought to be, or should not be. Have them use slide film and whatever kinds of cameras they have or can obtain. What is important is what they see and photograph, and what their photos mean to them.

When they have completed the photo assignment and have had the slides processed, ask them to go through their slides and select the photos that most speak to them of what the Church is, might be, or should not be. Then challenge them to create a slide sound show that reveals their ideas and feelings about the Church. Music might be used, actual voices or sound effects, as well as a narrator or several narrators.

If the show is appreciated by them, suggest that they invite their parents to a viewing followed by discussion.

2. *Make a Cultural Analysis:* Divide your group into three teams. One will consider the spoken word, the second the written word (manuscripts), and the third the printed word. Have them imagine that they are Christians living during the period where the whole culture centered on the spoken word, the written word, or the printed word. Have them discuss the consequences this might have on the Church. What difference would it make to the Church, what effect would it have on the Church if the culture in which it existed communicated by spoken words, manuscripts or books? What are the implications of the Church's message, organization, mode of evangelizing, style of authority?

After sufficient discussion, they might create some kind of presentation of their findings—either a simple listing of conclusions or a more elaborate, creative form of expressing and sharing their conclusions. This exercise can be very helpful in raising awareness of the impact of cultural media of communications on the Church and its mission.

3. *Pray/Meditate:* Create a climate of quiet relaxation. Play some appropriate instrumental music, or a carefully selected hymn about the Church. Then read, or have someone read slowly and meditatively the story of the Tower of Babel in Genesis 11:1-9. Allow time for silent reflection. Then encourage the sharing of reflections on the reading—which is about the disruption of communications between peoples through their sinful rupture of communication with God. Invite someone else to read again slowly and meditatively the story of Pentecost in which the Holy Spirit restores communications among peoples through the gracious intervention of God in Jesus' death and resurrection, Acts 2:1-12. After silent reflection, invite the spring of ideas about the reading to flow from the group. Guide their discussion to center on the Church as a communication. End with a prepared or spontaneous prayer and a hymn.

Adult Level

1. *Picture the Church:* Divide the entire group into three working teams. Each team is to work on one sketch or portrait of the Church according to the three understandings of the Church described in this chapter as hierarchical-scholastic, biblical-kerygmatic, and secular-dialogic.

Appoint someone in the group to take notes as each team strives to fill out in more detail, the characteristics of each of these models. Then have each group present a portrait of the Church in some creative fashion. Three collages could graphically present the similarities and differences between these three ways of looking at the Church. Or three brief slide-sound presentations, or a mural with the three portraits in historical sequence, or a composite of all three in one great portrait of the Church with these three co-existing dimensions.

Once the work is done, allow for time to enjoy and talk further about these three ways of looking at the Church.

2. *Make Verbal-Visual Statements:* To explore the unique potentialities of verbal and non-verbal communication, it helps to try to translate a basic message from one medium to the other. What is suggested here for visual communication may apply as well to other forms of non-verbal communication such as music, gesture, movement, dance, spatial arrangement, architecture, symbol, etc.

Have the group—or smaller teams within the group—select either a picture that they feel really says something about life or agree on a statement about life they feel is important today. Depending on whether they start with the picture or the verbal statement they will then try to express the same message or insight in the complementary medium.

For example, if they begin with a photograph, their task is to come up with a verbal statement that says more or less exactly what the photo says. If they begin with the verbal statement they need to find or take a photo that expresses the same insight. In place of photos, other forms of visual art might be substituted, e.g., paintings, sculpture, drawing.

When they have created a verbal-visual statement that is harmonious and complementary in expressing a single insight, ask them to explore together the differences between the verbal and visual media of communication. Which do they find more meaningful and why? Which touches them most deeply?

After completing and discussing their task, invite them to read and discuss the article.

3. *Create Media:* After assimilating the principles stated in the article, invite the group—individually or in small teams to create a media statement. Their media creation may be as sophisticated or unsophisticated as they wish, but it should simply stimulate the kind of

in-depth appreciation described in this chapter. Any subject matter may be selected.

Once they have completed their work, have them share what they have done. After time to enjoy and appreciate one another's work, invite honest criticism—positive and negative—of their work in the light of the principles underlying the Church as multi-media. A first step in this critique would be to have the group attempt to articulate what they feel each creation attempts to communicate.

RESOURCES

Using Media is a set of ten 35mm color filmstrips accompanied by either cassettes or records, produced by Gerard A. Pottebaum of Treehaus Communications for ROA Films, 1696 N. Astor St., Milwaukee, Wis. 53202. The set provides philosophical principles and practical suggestions for the use of media in general and slides, films, filmstrips, television, posters, pictures, chalkboards, overheads, and books in particular.

Jewels and Junk: How to Find the Most Useful Audio-Visuals for Religious Education by Rev. William A. Dalglish is a helpful cassette recording from Ave Maria, Notre Dame, Ind. 46556.

Carl J. Pfeifer, *Photomeditations* (Thomas More Association, 180 N. Wabash Ave., Chicago, Ill. 60601) is a book of reflections on life's mysteries through photographs and words. *Photomeditations* are also available as slides, with printed reflections, from Mark IV Presentations, Attleboro, Mass. 02703.

Helpful resources for current information and practical helps on media are:

Mass Media Newsletter, 2116 N. Charles St., Baltimore, Md. 21218.

Religious Media Today, 432 Park Ave. South, New York, N.Y. 10016.

Cultural Information Service, 74 Trinity Place: Suite 407, New York, N.Y. 10006.

Film and Broadcasting Review, 1011 First Ave., N.Y. 10022.

Film Information, Room 858, 475 Riverside Dr., N.Y. 10027.

READINGS

Avery Dulles' presentation to the American Bishops 1971 Communications Institute was printed in *The New Catholic World,* January 1972, under the title "The Church as Multimedia," and in booklet form "The Church is Communications" by Multi-Media International, 947 Park St., Attleboro, Mass. 02703.

The Vatican's *Pastoral Instruction for the Application of the Second Vatican Ecumenical Council on the Means of Social Communication* is available from the United States Catholic Conference Publications Office, 1312 Massachusetts Avenue, N.W., Washington, D.C.

Babin, Pierre, ed. *The Audio-Visual Man,* provides principles and examples by an international team of media experts (Pflaum/Standard, 3121 Hamilton Avenue, Cincinnati, Ohio 45231).

Some theoretical and many very practical media helps are found in Celia Hubbard, ed., *Let's See, No. 1: The Use and Misuse of Visual Arts in Religious Education,* (Paulist/Newman Press, 545 Island Rd., Ramsey, N.J. 07446).

John Harrell gives suggestions for using, creating, finding, and evaluating media in *Basic Media in Education* (St. Mary's College Press, Winona, Minn. 55987).

Also, see and compare official current statements on the Church and media by both the U.S. and Canadian Bishops.

Carl Pfeifer

9

The Church as Sign of Hope

"The world has lost its bearings. Not that ideologies are lacking to give directions only that they lead nowhere. People are going around in circles in the cage of their planet, because they have forgotten that they can look up to the sky ... Because all we want is to live, it has become impossible for us to live. Just look around you!"

Eugene Ionesco, the founder of the theater of the absurd, expressed the above sad assessment of contemporary society at the opening of the Salzburg Festival in 1972.

I am also haunted by a recent conversation with a college student. He was bright, from a financially secure family, with an apparently promising future. But Jim was obviously not happy. His face betrayed a dull sadness. His eyes lacked sparkle. His tone of voice and every gesture suggested heaviness, emptiness. Jim had attempted suicide, but accidently survived.

Jim was hurting. So was I as I listened. It was no time for glib reassurances, glittering promises. He had embraced a number of movements—religious, social, humanitarian—and found them without meaningful direction for his life.

Jim is but one of hundreds of thousands of young people who look at life with dimmed eyes and dulled hearts. A recent survey of college students indicated that their most serious problem was that of life's apparent meaninglessness. The routine round of activities left them with a feeling of life's absurdity. Suicide has become an increasingly frequent occurrence on college campuses, and even among high school students.

Another survey of successful business men and women indicated similar results. Despite their success, they experienced an emptiness, a sense of meaninglessness, a lack of purpose. They felt their greatest need was to find some meaning for their lives.

It would seem that Eugene Ionesco may not be far off target. Perhaps we have in too many instances forgotten that we can look up to the sky. We have lost our idealism. We have lost hope in something or someone higher, greater than ourselves and our world—not necessarily outside our world, but greater than it. Without that point of reference, life easily becomes like a meaningless rat race. It is within that horizon of meaninglessness that we might well look at another model of Church.

Church: Sign of Hope

The Church has long seen itself as a sign of hope to the world. The model of the Church as a hope-filled sign to the world is closely related to the Church as sacrament.

Centuries before the coming of Jesus, God's chosen people, the Jews, considered themselves as a *sign of hope* to the nations. Jerusalem, with the Temple of God at its heart, rested on a mountaintop as an attractive sign of a people living in harmony and happiness under the rule of a loving God. The Jews dreamed of the day when all nations would stream to the mountain city to praise their God and to find meaning, peace, justice, joy and hope.

The prophet Isaiah gives classic expression to this attractive image of God's people drawing all peoples to their mountain city (Isaiah 2:2-5). His attractive portrait is found in almost identical terms in the words of the prophet Micah. Micah adds the peaceful image of each person sitting "under his own vine or under his own fig tree, undisturbed." He also draws a picture of universal physical and social well-being (Micah 4:1-7). The image of God's people as a symbol of hope in a dark, warring, frustrated world has deep roots in our Judaeo-Christian heritage. It is closely related to the image of God's kingdom or reign—which God Himself is initiating. That kingdom is to be marked by peace and justice, joy and universal love, profound harmony between people and nature.

Jesus grew up with the ideals of Isaiah and Micah. His preaching drew upon their images. He went about the towns and villages of His country with the awesome message that the long awaited reign of God was at hand (Mark 1:15). He proclaimed that the hoped for kingdom of peace, joy, justice, love and wholeness was near—indeed it was already mysteriously present, like yeast hidden in a batch of bread dough.

To Jesus' listeners, His words sparked biblical images of swords beaten into plowshares, lions resting with lambs, contented families sitting beneath their own vines or trees, blind people seeing, lame people leaping with joy, and anxious people at peace. Wherever Jesus went, people recognized signs of God's kingdom in their midst and they yearned for the full coming of God's reign. Jesus was a moving sign of hope to thousands of men and women who opened their minds and hearts to Him. He gave them a glimpse of what life could really be like where the gentle power of God's presence brought people to live justly and compassionately, in wholeness of body and spirit.

After Jesus' death and resurrection, with the outpouring of His Spirit at Pentecost, His disciples gradually came to believe that they were to carry on the hope-giving mission of Jesus. They reinterpreted the scriptures, taking the imagery of the prophets as applying to the growing Church. The Church was the new Jerusalem. They were God's new people. Jesus Himself was the true Temple. They experienced God's reign in their midst and proclaimed its coming to the far reaches of the Roman Empire. Their lives and their message were essentially one of hope, of the triumph of life over death, grace over sin. They were heralds of the fullness of the kingdom to come, a kingdom already alive in their midst.

Down through the centuries, the Church has viewed itself as a sign of hope, a sign of God's reign among humanity. The Church's relation to and understanding of God's kingdom has differed from age to age. But through all the fluctuations of interpretation, Christians have remained aware that they were called to be a sign of hope to others, that they were to play an important role in the coming of God's reign throughout the world. Even when they failed to live up to their ideals, they never forgot that they—the Church—were to be the city on a mountain top, spreading light and warmth to all the world, drawing all peoples to the kingdom of their God.

Down through 20 centuries, the Church has been for millions of people in the most harrowing of circumstances, a profound sign of hope, meaning and purpose. Early Christian communities helped revitalize the decadent Roman Empire. Later the Church was a bulwark of hope as barbarian hordes overran Europe. It was the Church that largely inspired Europe through its dark age.

Christians reached out to the castoffs of the Roman Empire much the same as Christians continue to reach out to the outcast pariahs of India. The Church provided hope and purpose to peoples persecuted and oppressed in the past as it continues to do to millions behind the Iron Curtain today. And in our own country, the churches were a major factor in helping Blacks move from slavery to freedom to equality. Hundreds of thousands of Americans still find in the Church the focus of their lives, the ground for hope for a better world and for a new heaven and a new earth hereafter.

Ideal Realized

It is this ideal, partially realized down through the Church's history, that Vatican Council II holds up as a challenge to the Church today. The council repeatedly describes the *Church as a sign of hope*—in language less moving than that of Isaiah and Micah and Jesus, but none the less challenging.

The goal of the Church's life of fellowship and service is that "men throughout the world will be aroused to a lively hope—the gift of the Holy Spirit—that they will finally be caught up in peace and utter happiness in that fatherland radiant with the splendor of the Lord" (*Church in World,* 93).

The Church, therefore, continues to see itself as a sign of hope for the betterment of human life under the reign of a gracious God. By its life and its words, the Church is to draw people to itself as an attractive model of what human life can be at its finest, while pointing beyond itself to even greater expectations of wholeness and holiness.

That is the ideal, an ideal partially realized in most periods of the Church's history. God's reign has indeed been recognized in Christian communities which in turn gave real hope to those among whom they lived. But honesty demands that we admit that the Church as sign of hope has often been at best an ambiguous sign. At times, the Church has appeared more as a symbol of oppression and regression than of hope.

Today, despite many indications of remarkable renewal, we find more and more people—including good Catholics—looking elsewhere for signs of hope. There seems to be a dramatic shift away from the Church in its institutional, organizational forms. Few of the great forces for social change and human betterment find their inspiration in the Church. Few futurologists foresee the Church as a major factor in the development and improvement of society.

We are faced within the Church with a heightened awareness of our mission to be a sign of hope to a confused world, while fewer and fewer people appear to look to the Church for hope—at least for a better world. At a time when meaninglessness is so vast a problem, and when we claim to have the key to life's meaning, we seem often incapable of communicating hope to so many of our fellow citizens.

Perhaps one of the major challenges facing the Church today is to take a serious look at its own image and lifestyle. How can we become the effective signs of hope we are called to be? What is it about our lives that dims the light of Christ that shines all too weakly through us? Why is it that people like Jim, crushed by life's meaninglessness, fail to find hope in Christ's Church? How can we help people remember their ability to look up to the sky, recapture high ideals, rediscover purpose and meaning? What can the Church do to help people break out of the cage of directionless roaming?

The council sets down for the Church, for each Christian, an awesome challenge. "We can justly consider that the future of humanity lies in the hands of those who are strong enough to provide coming generations with reasons for living" (*Church in World,* 31).

SUGGESTED ACTIVITIES

Primary Level

1. *By Painting Rocks:* Give the children a large selection of small stones. Let each select one. Then have them feel how solid the rock is. Let them try to dent it, push against it. Let them feel its firmness and solidity.

Then lead them in talking about these qualities of rock that give security, e.g., the fact that tremendous buildings rest firmly on rock, the hugh rocks and rocky mountains withstand the strongest winds and storms, etc.

Share with them in very simple terms Jesus' words to Peter that upon this rock (Peter's faith in God) He would build His Church and nothing could ever destroy it. Let the children know that Jesus is that securing rock.

Have them then paint some symbol of Jesus on their individual rock. Perhaps pray with them part of one of the Psalms that calls God, "rock": Psalm 18, 62, 89, 95. Have them take their rock home as a reminder of how they can hope and trust in God, "our rock."

2. *Memorize prayers:* Share with the children phrases from the Psalms like "With you I shall always be," (Psalm 73:23), "God is the rock of my heart" (Psalm 73:26), "My God, my rock of refuge, my shield," (Psalm 18:3), "With God is my safety ... Trust in Him at all times," (Psalm 62:8-9), "You are my Father my God, the Rock, my savior," (Psalm 89:27).

Help them memorize one or more of the brief prayers. Then lead them in prayer, perhaps using pictures or slides of large solid rocks as a visual help to feeling the security of being with God.

3. *Plant seeds:* Provide each child with some kind of flower seed and a small pot in which to plant it. Or just have one larger pot and one seed for the whole group.

Water it.

Then over the weeks, keep watch with the children over the pot, noting any signs of life. When the seed first begins to break through the ground, have a little celebration with the children.

When the flower or plant is more fully developed, talk with the children about their experience with the seed. Help them feel something of the sense of expectation and its fulfillment in the actual flower or plant.

Then talk with them about Jesus and His Church. His death leads to new life for Him and others. The Church, too, is at times crushed, weakened, buried, but with Jesus it brings forth new life. Pray a prayer of hope.

Note: Even more dramatic would be to observe the emergence of a butterfly.

Intermediate Level

1. *Visualize a Psalm:* Share with the youngsters a psalm of hope and trust, like Psalm 73. You may want to select portions or simplify it if you feel your youngsters may find the language too difficult.

Have them study the Psalm carefully, perhaps in small groups. Ask them to note how they think the Psalmist feels, what problems he may be having, what is his chief source of hope, and why he turns to God for hope.

After they have considered the Psalm, ask them to visualize it, either by putting slides with it or by drawings or paintings, or works of art.

Let them share what they have created. Guide them to relate this to the Church, through which they come into contact with the Psalm and with people who share the same faith in God.

2. *By writing letters:* Suggest that the youngsters write letters to an imaginary pen pal or to a real friend in need. Have them select or imagine someone who is very discouraged with serious problems. Then ask them to write to that person words of hope. Their letters

could draw upon their own experience as well as on anything they have observed or learned, particularly through the Church or from the Bible.

3. *By Completing Sentences:* Write in large letters, "Hope is . . . . ." Invite the youngsters to complete the sentence. Then have them share what they have written.

As they talk about hope, guide them to search for signs of hope in what they know of the Church and committed Christians.

3. *Dream:* Create a comfortable atmosphere, with music and a relaxed situation. Invite the group to dream of an ideal world. Then have them articulate their dream either in words or through other media.

Encourage them to share their dreams. Then challenge them to consider what the Church—and what individual or groups of Christians—can do to help bring about the dream. If necessary, you might want them to evaluate or critique their dreams in the light of what they know about the Gospel and Jesus.

Challenge them to be as practical and realistic as possible. End with a prayer and perhaps listening to "The Impossible Dream" from *Man from La Mancha.*

Secondary Level

1. *Pray/Meditate:* Invite the group to meditate on the experience of meaninglessness and the image of the Church as a sign of hope to the world.

If possible, darken the room. Perhaps play some contemporary song suggesting meaninglessness or some background instrumental music that suggests a mood of restlessness, emptiness.

Have someone read aloud slowly the words of Ionesco at the beginning of this chapter. Allow some moments for silent meditation.

Then brighten the room, perhaps just with a candle. You might play some joyful music as background. Ask

someone to read the words of Isaiah 2:2-5 or the similar words of Micah 4:1-7. Again allow time for quiet
reflection.

Afterwards invite spontaneous prayer, perhaps initiating the prayer period with a spontaneous prayer of
your own.

Close with a hope-filled hymn or song.

2. *List Signs:* Share with the group the ideas in the
chapter. Then challenge them to think and talk about
the Church as they know it, with a view to coming up
with a list of indications that the Church does, in fact,
offer hope to people inside the Church and outside it.

Have them work in small teams and list their observations on newsprint. Then let each team share its list
with the rest of the group. Invite the whole group then
to try to arrive at a consensus listing composed of what
all would accept from the various lists. Then guide
them in talking about the Church realistically as a sign
of hope.

3. *Study Texts:* Take a closer look at some of the biblical and ecclesial texts cited or suggested in this chapter. Divide the group into small working teams. The following texts might be considered: Isaiah 2:2-5 and
Micah 4:1-7 (almost exact duplicates); Luke 4:16-22
and Matthew 11:1-6 (signs of God's reign); Documents
of Vatican II: *Church,* 1; *Church in World,* 45, 93.

In studying the documents, the teams might try to
keep these questions in mind:

What are characteristics of God's reign or kingdom?

To be a sign of hope in the kingdom of God, what
characteristics must the Church manifest?

After the teams have sufficiently explored their own
text(s), invite them to share their insights with the
whole group.

4. *Test reality:* Suggest that the group test this new
model of the Church against the real Church as they
know it. This may be done individually, in small teams,
or together as one large group.

Adult Level

1. *Analyze Models:* It may provide a helpful review as well as suggest new insights into the final model, that of "sign of hope," by considering each of the models specifically in search of aspects which suggest the Church is a sign of hope.

Divide the whole group into working teams, each to select for consideration one of the models proposed— *Pilgrim People, Institution, Sacrament, Herald, Servant, Worshipper,* etc. Have them recall, perhaps even reread the chapter on their model, the main points of the model. They' are then to examine that model carefully to discover how it reveals the Church as *a sign of hope.* It might be helpful for the teams to write down their discoveries on large sheets of newsprint.

From what all have discovered, the whole group might then create a sheet of characteristics of the *Church as sign of hope.* Once the portrait is completed, assess it in relation to the group's actual perception of the Church today. In this way a positive kind of creative critique can be carried out that would help the group discover signs of hope in the Church as it actually exists today.

RESOURCES

Cardinal Leo Suenen's views on how Christians can prepare for the future while remaining faithful to tradition are available on a NCR cassette, "The Church Between Yesterday and Tomorrow" (NCR Cassettes, Dept. CCW6, P.O. Box 281, Kansas City, Mo. 64141).

READINGS

Hans Küng explores in considerable length and depth the unique contribution of Christianity to the contemporary world of humanism and world religions in his monumental book *On Being Christian* (New York: Doubleday, 1976).

Carl Pfeifer

Epilogue

We have come a long way from the simpler days of my childhood in Blessed Sacrament parish on St. Louis' Northside. Our experience of life in general and of the Church in particular has changed dramatically. So it is not surprising that our once tidy definition of the Church as a "perfect society" has become a bit more messy—just as the reality of "church" has lost its look of uniformity. Pluralism and change today mark the one Church of Christ.

But what we have lost in neatness and clarity, we have gained in richness and depth. Our experience of Church and our descriptions of this faith community have gradually shifted from the external and observable toward the spiritual and experiential. As we have groped through much confusion and pain, we have found signs of the Holy Spirit's guiding presence to reassure us that deep unity can exist together with deeply felt differences, and that continuity of tradition is preserved only through development.

Efforts to describe or define the Church have likewise shifted from clear and distinct concepts to more symbolic and evocative images. As we have rediscovered the Church as mystery—a divine-human reality—our words have become somewhat more poetic than philosophic. Poetic images, recovered from the Scriptures, are at the heart of the more scientifically refined "models" of the Church which we have considered in the preceding chapters. Today it is realized better that the Church, like a precious multifaceted gem, is more than the sum of its measurable components.

The process of further refining the models of the Church necessarily continues. We have considered the five basic models proposed by Avery Dulles— *Mystical Communion or Pilgrim People, Institution, Sacrament, Herald, Servant*—and four further images— *Context of Faith, Multi-Media, Worshipper,* and *Sign of Hope.* No doubt others could be added in an attempt to find models that more adequately interpret the reality of Church and more fruitfully suggest new avenues of living and understanding Church.

Each of these models has strengths and weaknesses in helping us grasp and live what the Church really is. They are like the many facets of a diamond. Each makes its contribution toward the beauty and value of the whole. There is no "super-model" embracing them all in a clear and precise definition. Nor are all the models equally helpful. But together they provide a much richer, more pregnant and honest view of the Church than does the definition of Baltimore and Bellarmine.

Perhaps one could take one of these basic models and make it one's foundational model for understanding the Church. Into it, then, would be blended the vital values from the other models. In this way a more cohesive, comprehensive, image of the Church emerges. Dulles selects the "Sacrament" model for his personal foundation, but exemplifies how another, for example, "Servant," might also serve as the foundational model.

Only the "Institution" model—the one closest to that of Bellarmine and Baltimore—seems inadequate as a foundation. It least embraces and reveals the element of mystery, the reality of grace uniting all members with God and with one another in Christ Jesus through the power of the Holy Spirit.

The approach through models has been helpful in understanding the contemporary and traditional reality of the Church and the biblical, traditional, and modern interpretations of that reality. It has also been fruitful in catalyzing more creative, more effective forms of ecclesial life. Definitions interpret already existing reality but they also help shape emerging reality. It is therefore no mere academic exercise to work through one's presuppositions about the Church.

All of us—aided by competent theological experts and legitimate ecclesial leaders—have the demanding challenge of rethinking our understanding of the Church. Such rethinking needs to be rooted in our experience of Church and the Holy Spirit. It is a process requiring prayer and dialogue as well as reflection and research.

Undoubtedly the experience and understanding of Church will continue to develop. Avery Dulles suggests that the Church will be more and more marked by (1) *modernization of structures,* (2) *ecumenical interplay,* (3) *internal pluralism,* (4) *provisionality,* and (5) *voluntariness.* Karl Rahner has a similar list of five characteristics of the Church of the near future. He sees the Church as more (1) *democratized,* (2) *ecumenical,* (3) *open,* (4) *critical of the socio-political order,* and (5) *grounded in voluntary base communities.* Other theologians have their own projections. No doubt each Catholic has his or hers.

In a developing Church within a changing world, it is imperative that our own individual insights and feelings be tested against the community of believers. St. Paul points out that all are gifted by the Spirit for the building up of the community, the Church. He teaches that within the community there are complementary gifts. In today's Church, there are three uniquely gifted groups whose gifts need to be allowed free interaction.

Most important of all three are *the faithful* of all ages and backgrounds. They have the rich giftedness of living and attempting to make sense out of Church where Church primarily happens—at home and in the local parish. Among them are some whose education and training suggest a special giftedness. These are experts like *theologians.* Finally, and no less important, are those called to lead the community—the *priests, bishops and pope.*

It is only through the honest interaction of *the faithful, the experts* and *the leaders* that the Church today— as in previous historical eras—develops its authentic experience of the Holy Spirit and its own understanding of itself as Church.

With genuine dialogue, it can be expected that whatever direction the Church grows in the future, it will do so in continuity with its tradition and in ever-deepening unity that can embrace legitimate differences.

In the process of creative dialogue, the example and words of Pope John and Vatican Council II are a sound guide: "Let there be unity in what is necessary, freedom in what is unsettled, and charity in any case."

The Author

Carl J. Pfeifer, respected theologian, writer, educator and photographer is known for his syndicated column in NC News and for a wide variety of published works. Among these are the newly released *Silver Burdett Religious Education Program* (co-authored with Janaan Manternach), *Photomeditations,* and *A Book For All Seasons.*

He is currently working on other books and filmstrip projects from his home in Arlington, Virginia.